HQ759.L63

LOWE
THE CRUEL STEPMOTHER

WITHDRAWN FROM THE EVAN'S
LIBRARY AT FMCC

DATE DUE			
MAY 10 1972			
F/S/ 76			
NOV 19 02			

GAYLORD M-2 · PRINTED IN U.S.A.

FULTON-MONTGOMERY COMMUNITY
COLLEGE LIBRARY

The Cruel Stepmother

The Cruel Stepmother

by
Patricia Tracy Lowe

Prentice-Hall, Inc.
ENGLEWOOD CLIFFS, N. J.

Designed by Linda Purnell

The Cruel Stepmother
by Patricia Tracy Lowe
© 1970 by Patricia Lowe Pitzele
Copyright under International and Pan American
Copyright Conventions
All rights reserved. No part of this book may be
reproduced in any form or by any means, except
for the inclusion of brief quotations in a review,
without permission in writing from the publisher.
ISBN 0-13-194936-5
Library of Congress Catalog Card Number: 74-114685
Printed in the United States of America T
Prentice-Hall International, Inc., London
Prentice-Hall of Australia, Pty. Ltd., Sydney
Prentice-Hall of Canada, Ltd., Toronto
Prentice-Hall of India Private Ltd., New Delhi
Prentice-Hall of Japan, Inc., Tokyo

The  Families

Pat Joplin, (formerly Mrs. Pat Links), THE CRUEL STEPMOTHER

Noah Joplin, Pat's second husband

Andrew Joplin, natural child of Cora and Noah Joplin, Pat's stepchild

Nicholas and Samuel Links, natural children of Pat Joplin and Martin Links, and Noah's stepchildren

Cora Joplin, Noah's former wife, natural mother of Andrew

Martin Links, Pat's former husband, natural father of Nicholas and Samuel

Ann Links, Martin's second wife, stepmother of Nicholas and Samuel, and natural mother to three children, Martin's "second family"

This book is dedicated to them all

The  Cruel Stepmother

I

This is a book about the life of a stepmother. Me. What it describes are the daily happenings, the excitements, the dishwashing boredom of routine, the crises, the peak moments of hilarity and delight, the feet-sucking bogs of depression and inadequacy almost impossible to bear, that are the experience of most mothers blessed with husband and children. In our family there was a difference. Coming into this, my second marriage, I brought two sons, Nicholas and Samuel Links, aged 6 and 4. My new husband, Noah Joplin, contributed his son, Andrew, aged 8. Thus there confronted each other five persons, between them encompassing these relationships: husband and wife; father-stepmother; mother-stepfather; father-son; mother-sons; stepfather-stepsons; stepmother-stepson; and finally brothers-stepbrother or brother-stepbrothers. Enough to bewilder any adult, let alone a child. So while the components of this family pudding for the most part differed little from those of other families, the problems loomed larger than normal and there were more of them. The feelings of its members were accordingly more intense. Self-consciousness was there, and resentments were inevitable.

My stepson Andrew is now in his late twenties, an associate professor of Comparative Literature at an Eastern university.

His blood mother is ill, and has been for many months. Because there is no one else to do so, he has assumed full responsibility for her care. And so the gradual sloughing off of childhood's skin, the high-spirited fun and games, the irresponsibility, the careless outlook on life till one chooses to live otherwise, ended for him with a bump. For this young man who during adolescence had been slow to mature, there was no longer possible the leisurely two steps forward, one step back reaching towards responsibility that marks the human condition at this stage in the game. Andrew is serious now, highly sensitized, tense, often withdrawn into introspection about his problems. Today he is able, however, to make the switch necessary for normal exchange with others. A child cannot do this. A childish adult cannot do this, or a boy emerging from the chrysalis of adolescence. Andrew today is able to cope with the inordinately difficult and the humdrum alike. So I know my stepson is a man.

And yet, although he has been married since he was 23, had before that lived away at college five years (one year studying abroad), and spent four at boarding school, thus apart from his father and me, and separated (except for holidays spent sometimes with his mother, sometimes with us) from the "relationship" problem for thirteen years, our resentments are still there. I mean his resentment towards me and mine towards him.

I make an assertion here, one that I believe bears repeating, that more often than not the resentment between stepparent and stepchild *never* goes away. That is, of course, if these two people have and maintain any kind of meaningful relationship at all through the years. It doesn't matter how much love, liking, respect, admiration, or real friendship (and several of these qualities exist in Andrew's and my relationship) there is. I would almost say the more there are of these elements in the relationship, the more likely there is to be resentment at the drop of a hat as well. The resentment that was present during their earliest days together can return in a flash of instant hostility, touched off perhaps by the most trivial of matters. It is precisely because at the beginning of the relationship of these two people they resented each other's presence, they do so now when the surface is scratched. As in the beginning they wished the other elsewhere, or nonexistent, they do so now—when resentment flares. But it is also true that if the basic feelings between them rest on solid foundations, are real and good, when there is any sort of crisis or serious need for help by one of them the response by the other is likely to be immediate and the resentment forgotten.

Of course a son may and often does resent his blood father; a daughter her mother, even more a son his mother and a daughter her father. But somehow there is a different quality to this resentment, and the time span in which it exists is usually finite instead of permanent. Certainly the element of self-consciousness is not likely to be present. Perhaps it is the very knowledge of the step-relationship itself, its essential wrongness as dictated by our Puritan ethics and set of rules, that accounts for the difference. I am not sure. But different it is, this resentment, and it is manifested in different ways.

I will give two examples. As I mentioned earlier, Andrew's mother has been ill. During the worst moments of this illness Andrew came to our house to discuss matters with his father, who was the only "older" person (there is no one in his mother's family) to whom he could turn for advice—and also comfort. Forced to spend a great deal of time telephoning innumerable doctors, he did this also from the house—my house. This was all necessary. My home is Andrew's home when he is in town. But after the first days and weeks of crisis were over, I minded the unavoidably intimate way Noah continued to be involved. We all were, and I resented it. What sense was there to this, though? I was not threatened in any way. Yet the continual reminder of it all, the necessary dealing with the day-to-day problems of Andrew's mother, was something I could not cope with rationally and objectively. The sense of crisis, of tragic circumstance, became buried beneath petty attitudes and consequent guilty conscience.

The other situation occurred one night recently when my husband and I sat in our living room with two close friends. We had eaten well and were full of bonhommie, good cheer, and good talk. Andrew entered the room, greeted everyone, and joined in the discussion with as much pleasure and good humor as everyone else. Greeted everyone, that is, but me. He did not even look in my direction for about half an hour. Then he included me with the others, in perfect equanimity and with no chip on his shoulder against me. The reason? He had come from visiting his mother and resented my presence. I should not have been there, even after twenty years or so. When his mind took over from his unthinking reaction and his body untensed from its posture of meeting crises, I was once more included in the group, once more a member of his society. I doubt, however, whether my stepson's feelings will ever be translated into action against me, in the way of a man from Nairobi, Kenya, who bit off part of his stepmother's left ear, was ordered to receive eight strokes of the cane and was sentenced to a year in prison.

As I began to get down to the writing of this book, which I have been thinking about and puttering over for a long time now, I decided to ask the three boys themselves what they remembered from their days of stepchildhood as being particularly memorable and/or disturbing. What event, what scene, what attitude or aspect of our lives (and in Nick and Sam's case, their lives with their other family too, since their father had remarried and they had a stepmother and in time a half sister and two half brothers added to their stew of relationships) did they find especially difficult?

Nick is overseas in the Peace Corps and Sam is working in another town. I did write to each and ask, but sheer distance makes it difficult to extract a response from either of them. But one morning when Andrew was in town and we sat dallying over coffee, I put the question to him. Andrew, while professionally involved in much that is over my head, is essentially and by avocation a teacher. He likes to talk, to explain, and he does both well, easily, and with simplicity. He did not hesitate.

"It was the Saturday night syndrome, you might call it," he said. "Our weekly indoor picnic, cooking hot dogs over the living-room fire. It says it all, right there. The things I did to make Dad and you fight, the whole bit."

"What are you saying? I don't understand," I said, stirring my coffee furiously.

"The more I could make Dad get angry and you cry, the better I liked it," he answered.

Even in this late date in our lives together, and even though I must have known all this, and had even hashed the scenes over and over to myself, I was shocked. Perhaps because it was articulated so frankly.

"Go on," I said.

"All kids want that, if their parents split up. At least, all the ones I've talked to do, and that's quite a few. They all agree with me. They want their real parents back together again, no matter how *that* was, good or bad, and they do everything they can to destroy the new arrangement." Andrew banged his coffee cup down in the saucer and looked at me. "All of them. Or at least all of them think about it, even if they can't actually do anything about it—stir things up, I mean."

He was categoric (Andrew nearly always speaks aggressively, with emphasis, but this time more so than usual). "If you can put this across in your book," he continued, "you'll be making a contribution, because that's the scene, that's the way it really is."

"But Nick wasn't like that," I said. All of me was protesting this idea—not that kids want their parents back together again, but that a 9-year-old or a 7-year-old could be so deliberately destructive.

"Nick didn't need to be. I did it for him. I bet it's what he wanted to do, just the same."

I felt stunned. Later in the day I shared the whole conversation with a friend of mine with two daughters, who also had been married for the second time. Honestly, I expected to hear her tones of horror over the telephone equal mine. On the contrary.

"He's right," she told me. "Mary was like that."

"Mary!" Mary is a demure-seeming gentle girl, an artist and model, a bit outré, but *nice*.

"Sure. Mary. Believe it. Whenever she visited James on a weekend, she'd come back and tell me if it had been a success or not. And in her view, a success meant making her stepmother cry. She was most explicit about it. I remember vividly." My friend's voice rose slightly. "It made me want to throw up. I took to my bed, out of horror at my daughter—and my own guilt, perhaps. Mary had to look after me."

"I think that's terrible," I said. "Do you believe *all* stepchildren are so destructive? So angry, and vindictive, almost?"

"I'm sure they all want to be, at least for a time. Anyway, I don't know that it's destructive or vindictive. It is a protest, I guess, and they *are* angry, for which you can hardly blame them."

I sighed. "Perhaps I won't do the book after all," was all I could muster by way of response.

A week later there came in the mail a letter from Nick in Asia. He began: "I find myself very reluctant. . . ." It was *his* answer to my query about his early years. He was reluctant—but not that reluctant, since he did go on. I too am reluctant, because the words I read in that flimsy blue air-letter, like Andrew's spoken ones, were shocking to me, and, because of what they imply, disturbing to say the least. However, I too will go on; I quote him:

"I am now 24 years old, and I have still not gotten over my extreme discomfort at my two families meeting each other. I would like to keep these worlds completely separate. Consequently, in addition to not wishing to talk—for the purposes of a (*literary*) project—about Noah and you, I don't want to talk to you about my father or Ann either. So, all I can do is make a few very general remarks. . . . My feelings towards Noah and Ann, my stepfather and stepmother, were indifferent (this is in the early years). I did not feel much of anything for either of them. I did not fight them. I adapted to them. I hated you, and idealized my father. I wanted to live on Long Island rather than in Brooklyn. I was acutely conscious of seething with emotion. I wanted to get out of that house. Also . . . I have felt that the burden of suffering placed on me because of the divorce legitimized any emotions I might have. The divorce left me to my own emotional defenses and consequently I did not feel responsible to parents—the agents of my suffering—for those attitudes I adopted while coping. . . . To a certain extent this feeling is still with me. For example, because of the past,

I am shattered by parental discord—between you and Noah, my father and Ann (in fact any conflict arouses in me a strong emotional reaction). Shakespeare has Juliet's father say, when he sees his daughter lying lifeless in the vault, 'How could she do this to me?' In instance after instance I have observed since my boarding school days that parents are prone to selfishness. All individuals, to be sure, are egocentric. The trouble is that kids don't expect this in their parents, and a divorce, perhaps, with the remarriages and personal adjustments which usually follow, strikes the child as parental selfishness of the harshest kind. . . . I might add, in ending these unsatisfactory thoughts, that I have always told people when discussing my situation, that it couldn't have worked out better. And I appreciate, the particular difficulties notwithstanding, that the clue to this success is the restraint which my four parents have practiced."

Our divorce, it appears, affected these two boys somewhat differently. One wished to create discord, to return to the *status quo ante.* The other, outwardly accepting of the situation (although Andrew's belief that all children in this situation wish to break up the present relationship to return to the previous one is probably valid), was shattered by discord. What had we done to these boys?

There is no forcing or structuring of occasions to talk about problems in the past. Sam's answers to my question were supplied at a later time, and appear in the final chapter.

Years ago, when I first started thinking about and working on this book, I naturally read Dr. Louise Despert's *Children of Divorce*. I was most struck by her words (perhaps because in them I found a sort of absolution, a confirmation, a validation of what I feared secretly might be rationalization?): "Divorce is not automatically destructive to children," she wrote; "the marriage which divorce brings to an end may have been more so." I had acted in this belief myself.

But after reading Nick's letter, I wondered as I had a thousand times before, whether Noah and I should not better have lived out our less than satisfactory first marriages because the conflicts, dissensions and frustrations in them might have been more "normal," less hurtful to our children.

But we did "live through" divorce; and we did remarry. I cannot help asking myself what I had done or left undone, to help Andrew, Nicholas, and Sam in these troubling years. What had I managed to solve? I had for the most part felt unsure, ineffective, and often sorry for myself, if not consciously filled with guilt. Would I be able to rehash all of this, and dwell on it enough to produce a book?

I thought about it some more. They interest me, these turbulent evocations of the past. I find them disturbing, but stimulating, too. The story gnaws away at me, is always present at the back of my mind. Of course, for me it is not yet at an end. Perhaps what happened to us and how we reacted will have meaning to others. It will give them tough, rough food to digest, complex problems to ponder. But it might be of help. I am doing the book.

II

"Stepmothers are mean."

Most of our children believe this. So if you are a stepmother, or are about to become one, don't delude yourself that your stepchild does now or will in the future look upon you as his mother. He won't. The necessary chemistry just isn't there. Instead, he is possessed of a demon myth.

Down through many centuries and many cultures—our Western culture is not alone in this by any means—have come tales of the evil, cruel stepmother. The point of the stories has become deep-rooted as a concept, and it is now firmly embedded in the minds of our children. Whether or not they have read Hans Christian Andersen, the Brothers Grimm, Mother Goose, or the Arabian Nights, children believe that stepmothers are cruel or wicked. The words actually flow together, in their minds, and are spoken in one breath: cruelstepmother. And so what has evolved is that cruelty, meanness, and even wickedness are implicit in the word itself. *Stepmother* means to most of us a person with a cruel, unpleasant, and unnatural attitude towards children. And *stepchild* has come to mean a person or thing treated less well, one in an inferior, shunted-to-one-side position.

For example, a farmer will refer to the runt of a litter as the "stepchild" of the batch; the Labor Department used to be known (not any more, I venture) as the "stepchild" of the government; why a pansy, that beautiful velvety purple and yellow flower should be called *stieffmütterchen* or "little stepmother" in Germany, I do not know. (Here is a German gardening encyclopedia's explanation of this odd piece of lore: "Of the five petals in a pansy, two are stepchildren, with only one 'chair' or sepal to sit on between them; two are non-stepchildren, and with a 'chair' or sepal apiece; and the mother sits on two 'chairs,' or sepals, of her own!")

Of the more than 70 million children in the United States as of 1968, at least 700,000 were "children of divorce." Divorce is today a commonplace; on the surface it is no longer considered a social oddity, or, in the urban centers at least, a shameful thing. You will find in application blanks to schools and colleges these days not only a space for the applicant to fill in his father's name and his mother's, but his stepfather's and stepmother's as well. But no matter how many of them there are, these children of divorced parents have all been hurt. If one of their parents remarries and they are thus stepchildren, they will be on the defensive at once. It is more than likely that they will act as children do when they are both hurt and on the defensive: they will carry a chip on their shoulder—and it will be one that is extremely hard to knock off. They are not going to be easy to love and care for, especially when the person caring for them, who is trying and hoping to love them, is an outsider. This outsider is replacing their real mother at their father's side. Automatically she will be looked upon as a stepmother—unhappily theirs—who, according to all that they have absorbed from their culture, from stories and attitudes, will unquestionably be unkind or even cruel to them.

Because of what is inherent in the situation and its relationships, it is more than likely that the stepmother will actually fulfill the role expected of her and *be* cruel. Even if by objective standards she is treating her stepchild exactly as she treats her own children—if she has them—from his point of view she is harsh and unfair. The tone of voice in which she reprimands him may be the same as the one she uses towards her own; but to him it sounds different. He may feel she is quicker to anger with him. And he is probably right. She *is* quicker to anger, but *after* making more effort to control it. She therefore is slower to show her anger; her self-consciousness about it all is enormous. When she finally does lose control, her resentment at the child for making her do so shows in her voice. Altogether the stepchild can make out a good case against his new "mother": she is an interloper, a usurper of power who has taken it upon herself to scold him, to tell him to pick up his clothes, wash his hands, and eat his spinach, who does not "understand," as his own mother does (or did) when he is naughty or obstreperous.

The fact that it is his father who has placed this person in a position to do these things is not admitted—is, rather, pushed out of his mind. Actually, it isn't likely that he'll blame his father for anything. Being like all children a realist, he knows he must have one ally in the house; and it makes sense that he chooses the familiar figure of his father, whom he loves and who loves him, for this role. Even if he had not been too close to him before the divorce of his parents, his father is what remains of the old life. Perhaps it is different with a girl in this situation; she might well be jealous, resentful of, and angry at her father. It was I, apparently, whom my son resented the most and not, as I thought at the time, his new stepfather. The differences in sexes and Oedipus must have bearing on this!

The sooner a woman contemplating marriage to a man with one or more children realizes that she cannot be a mother to them and understands some of the reasons, the sooner will she be able to provide a cheerful stable home for her new family, and herself bring an end to her own confusion, frustration, and despair at her climbing-up-the-wall feeling. I didn't know this. I hadn't a clue, to tell the truth. I didn't understand for a second that I *couldn't* replace Andrew's mother and shouldn't try. I had not worked out in my mind that the step-relationship is not a natural relationship, and never can be. That self-consciousness is always there. Of course, things go wrong in every household with considerable frequency when children and parents are growing up. But when they do in the complicated sort of setup we are talking about, the tensions and resentments thus triggered are far greater and much more difficult to dispel.

If the stepmother is kind and fair-minded, loving in nature and intelligent, the situation she finds herself in on remarriage is going to raise some very troubling emotions, doubts, and conflicts inside of her. Unless she is able to find some half-way satisfactory resolution for most of them, they can diminish her confidence in herself and ruin her serenity, and even her ability to function. They can damage her relationship with her own children. And at worst, they can, and often do, wreck her second marriage.

The stepchild faces the task of adjusting to his stepmother and readjusting to his father in a different role. And he must adjust to stepbrothers and stepsisters, if there are any. His reactions will be unthinking, from his gut—though probably so disguised as to be unrecognizable to the adults around him.

The stepmother has a far harder prospect ahead of her. Possessed, let us hope, of developed, disciplined thought processes, with their help she must not only adjust to the child, but to her new husband as well. She *must* make this marriage work. Having failed once (I talk of my own situation—obviously not all stepmothers were married before), the pressure on her will be great, and her fears and her sense of guilt will make this pressure seem even greater than it is. Besides giving her husband the morning-till-night proof of love that marriage demands (and remember that he, if she has children also of a previous partnership, is competing with them for her and is likely to be almost as "childish" about this competition as they are), she must also demonstrate continuously to herself and to everyone else, the fallacy of the stepmother image. She must not give it credence herself or she is lost before she has begun. Yet she must recognize the existence of the myth, its strength and vinelike tenacity, and she must deal with it realistically in spite of her temptation to brush it aside like a half-sensed cobweb, or sweep it under the rug like a curl of dust.

The important thing for her to realize from the beginning is that she is up against a very, very tough Everest sort of period in her life. There will be times when she feels hurt, rebuffed, misunderstood by husband and children—even her own. There will be occasions when she will be consumed by guilt because of unintentional pain she has caused—and if the stepmother myth has really got her, she may ask herself if this pain couldn't have been partly intentional, even if subconsciously so. She will perhaps not believe her eyes when for the first time her stepchild shows himself as adept as Andrew was at causing her and his father to bicker over him, even to quarrel bitterly. Worse, she may, like me, be so blind or stupid that she doesn't for a second see what it is that her stepchild is doing and thus in a way abdicates her adult powers to him where they should not be abdicated. She will be surprised or perhaps shocked when she stands up for child or stepchild against others, only to have the object of her concern resent her help and blandly reject it. She may find that she will have to make a choice between husband and children—either in a very basic way or in trivial matters and on many occasions.

Her new life will be a tough one for many reasons, but principally because everything—and I mean everything—depends on her. Most homes revolve around the mother; it is she who sets the tone and the climate for family spirits. When the children are of mixed parentage and the relationships therefore complex, this is even more emphatically the case. The stepmother's ability to cope with her problems with some sort of equanimity, the strength with which she can use her husband's love as fortifier, bear a very direct relationship to the happiness and serenity of the household as a whole.

Sometime between the reading of Cinderella and Cymbeline the stepmother concept is pushed far back in the subconscious mind. An adult is hardly aware of it. Even if this adult is on the verge of becoming a stepmother herself, it is still unlikely that she will give it any thought possessed of body and form. On the contrary, from the time she was able to read, a girl child has put herself firmly in the place of Cinderella vis-à-vis the two wicked stepsisters and stepmother. If, after the breakup of her first marriage, she has once again found her Prince Charming, she *still* does not doubt her own "niceness," the belief that *she* is the heroine. Approaching marriage for the second time to a man with children of his own, she will be counting on her own good sense, her love for the new husband, and perhaps an affection for children in general, to pull her through. She almost certainly has not identified herself with the wicked stepmother. But I am afraid this well-meaning but unconstructive approach is not good enough.

    I know, because this was my attitude. I went through debilitating self-doubt and anguished emotional conflicts. My marriage was not wrecked, though it came close to foundering many times. Like my son Nick, I too was torn apart by discord. I made the scene worse by watering it with tears that my children found upsetting and my stepson rewarding—both reactions destructive. There were disputes in the course of our daily lives, arguments galore, even open warfare. From all this Nick and Sam shrank into the shadows, while Noah and Andrew, it could fairly be said, thrived on the fire of battle and were not averse to fanning the flames.

Had I been younger and not failed once before, I might well have left and, figuratively speaking, run home to Mamma (this raises an important point: by and large partners in a second marriage are inclined to make more effort, put up with sharper hurts, and make more compromises—they want and need to succeed this time).

My stepson and my own two children were scarred, of course. But I do not think (and they seem to agree with me) they were scarred irreparably. They are satisfactorily operating human beings who are capable of loving and being loved. This surely is one of the more important criteria of maturity, and whether they still dislike and/or resent a stepparent doesn't matter very much. Today I believe they are all reasonably happy and successful in what they want to do, in spite of the unquestionable truth that the divorce of their parents was hard on them. As for me, I spent many years with little peace of mind and not much carefree enjoyment of my family life—and practically no serenity at all. I tried to be a mother to all—stepchild and children alike. And of course I wanted to be a good wife as well. It didn't work. It was just not possible. And so I was unhappy, and I believe much of the time everyone else was too.

On this spring day, as I sit writing in arcadia, where wild geese honk over our pond before finishing their journey north, my life is different indeed. This morning the swallows came; and when I inspected the peach tree and the plum, I could spot the tiny fruit already beginning to swell. I am able to enjoy all this. I have the time—and I have the peace of mind. There is at least a periodic serenity to my days, disturbed, yes, not too long ago by the youngest boy's visits home from college with ten friends (an exaggeration, but that's the way it seemed); a weekend with Andrew and talking half the night; a frantic buying, wrapping, and postal mailing spree to Nick in Asia (he'll get the packages sent at Christmas for his birthday in August) when I suddenly worry about his poor food and lack of reading matter.

During the years when the boys were growing up, a beleaguered father of four small sons would sometimes tell me how well behaved ours were, how bright and happy and fond of each other they all seemed, and what a great family we appeared to be to him. Self-consciously I would shrug off his words. They had no meaning to me even then, when I thought little and knew nothing (other than intuitively and instinctively—neither attitude to be dismissed out of hand) of what lay beneath the surface. Just yesterday a younger man, not so far along in child rearing, with a son of 10 living with the mother he had divorced, voiced similar compliments when he dined with Noah and Andrew. "Seeing how Andy is today," he said to my husband, "how close you are and how well he has turned out, gives me the greatest encouragement for Terry and his future."

But there can be no sense of smugness or satisfaction, really, in thinking back to the past. I remember too vividly Andrew's description of intentional discord-sowing and Nick's letter describing his feelings of hate, despair, and emotion that rent him apart. I don't think any one of us could feel a jot of self-satisfaction, for the years were too full of ups, downs, and roundabouts which, if one were able to pictograph them in some way, would resemble a roller coaster more than anything else. Rarely had a week or even a day gone by without some sort of crisis great or small, real or imagined. Were they happy ones, those years? Happy isn't the word exactly. Fulfilled, yes, though full of torment as well, of doubts and resentments, or suppressed emotions or too facilely expressed hurts, or explosions of anger. Would I do it

over again? *Today* I feel I would give much
to do it over, possessed, of course, of some of the
strength, knowledge, and experience that I have
now. One does learn, in time; of this I am sure.
One can perhaps grow a hide of rhinoceros and
develop the necessary backbone. *Tomorrow* I
might say, Heavens, No! Thank God it's over!
But if I were suddenly transported back in time
to the day it all began, I think I'd do it better now,
because I wouldn't kid myself that the impossible
was possible—I would accept my role of
stepmother, know it for what it was—and try to
be a good one.

III

Let me go back to the beginning of my second marriage. It was clear to Noah and myself that our children should not be presented with our marriage as a *fait accompli*, that if possible they should meet each other several times before the living together as a family was to take place, that the three boys should become friendly without friendship or stepbrotherhood being thrust down their throats.

   Noah had of course been to my apartment many times, filling the boys' heads with fantasy that he somehow managed to make part of their own daily lives. He told them, for example, of Nopki Walli and Oski-Moffy Shvoo Shvoo, who lived in the hot water pipes. When the not infrequent banging in the pipes could be heard in the apartment, it was the two of them arguing, or possibly coming to blows. Noah also maintained that he entered our fourth-floor apartment through the window. "But *how* did you get up here?" the boys would ask in astonishment (they never tired of the same tale told over and over again).

"By climbing up your mother's hair, like Rapunzel's," he answered. "Didn't you hear me calling her to let it down for me?" My hair is short and curly, but they more than half believed him anyway. I think he was mysterious to them, out of a storybook himself. It never crossed my mind that they might not like him. None of the stock words or concepts classic to the situation, such as rival, competition, jealousy, apprehension over mother's love and attention being diverted, came into my head. I just enjoyed believing that he was a figure of continual excitement for them. It seemed they could not get enough of him, the way they rushed to greet him, hugging his legs and clambering on his lap if he was rash enough to sit down. Actually they did not have more than a moment or two of his company, as we almost immediately left the house on a date as soon as he had entered it. For him, because they were not obstreperous and were well mannered and affectionate, they meant no trouble and gave him no fears of trouble to come. My life with them, though without a father at home, ran fairly smoothly at that time.

I had been separated from my husband for close to a year and worked at an office, with a live-in housekeeper whose pay ate up all my earnings and more, to the point where I was forced as well to correct manuscripts at night. Nick was then 5 years old, Sam 3. I was able without difficulty to leave them when I wanted to go out, without tantrums or pleadings. So Noah did not anticipate problems. I doubt that either of us thought the change in our lives that we were planning would represent anything but change for the better. As for me, the glory in the idea of life with Noah was overriding. It was what I wanted and so must be right. The rest was bonus. Love, companionship, the security of a 4-storied house, solidity, no worries about debts (I had plenty), dentists' bills, schooling—it was all too good to be true. But the completely prevailing emotion was my love and my need. There is absolutely no question that Nick's accusation of parental selfishness was at this point just. It was my need, not his, that consumed me. Dark thoughts of conflicts, jealousy, withdrawal, resentment were foreign to me, and certainly not in connection with Nick, up till then an unreserved, merry, loving child. He must have had them. Sam was little, under 3. I had not read the proper books.

During the eighteen months or so that Noah and I knew each other, during which both of us became divorced, obviously we saw each other a great deal. There was a black period for me in which Noah made an attempt to patch up his first marriage and returned to his home, to his wife and son. It did not work. He returned to his analyst (I had begun with one, during the dark days of my despair). Nothing changed our minds or hearts. We both gave it all the time in the world (me, willy-nilly); and Noah gave it thought and anguished appraisal of self and the others in his family. Not I. It never crossed my mind to weigh pros and cons. I only felt, and hoped, and prayed it would all come true. I have never ceased blessing my good fortune.

Noah took Andrew often to children's theater. He made a habit of it, and whenever the opportunity arose, off they went of a Saturday afternoon. So we thought that one such occasion would provide a fine, unstructured setting for the meeting of the boys—the three of them. It so happened that my English brother was staying with his family in New York at the time, and so we included them in the picture. I, with Nick and Sam, went to *Pinocchio* with my brother and two of his children, Noah with Andrew. We did not sit together. During intermission we greeted the other party as though our meeting were a thing of chance. That children are not very often taken in did not seem to have occurred to us.

When the play was over, we all went to Rumpelmayer's for a soda. I had already met Andrew, of course, but in those days he was not an outgoing boy, and I was reserved. No immediate rapport or intimacy had been achieved. And so we greeted each other, that was all. It was different with Nick and Sam. Freed of the restraints put on them by a crowded theater, and exhilarated by the crisp autumn air, they rushed up to Noah the minute they spied him among the parents and children pouring in a steady confluence of streams out of the lobby and swooped together to hug his knees in what, had they been bigger, would have had the effect of a football tackle. I caught sight of Andrew at that moment, standing apart, behind his father. He was silent, his head a bit on one side and the corners of his mouth downcurved. He wasn't appreciating what he saw at all, though obviously he didn't understand its implications—a threat to his whole way of life. None of this occurred to me at the time. I don't mean to imply that I was particularly callous or unkind. But I *was* unthinking.

In general this first meeting seemed to go off well (the ice cream sundae having cheered Andy up). Who's to know? I think now we really didn't do enough along the lines of bringing the children together so that they were at ease with one another. There were many possibilities in New York, where we all lived, as there are for that matter in any city, or the country as well. There is the zoo, often with a cafeteria (kids are immeasurably helped by the comfort of eating), plays, athletic events such as baseball games (we had the blessed Dodgers, of course, living in Brooklyn as Noah did), lunch at the Automat, trips to the beach, picnics, the circus, or basketball at Madison Square Garden.

But once the momentous news of the forthcoming merging of two families is dished up for children to digest, it is probably best not to resort to more of these pretty obvious stratagems, obvious even to small children. Strange as it seems, at this late date I cannot remember how I told my children of what the future held in store for them. I am sure there was not much made of it, though. I was not one to be emotional with them, and they did not ask many questions. I tended to play things down and be matter of fact. I *am* sure there was no problem and no sense of apprehension on their part, as there must have been on Andrew's. The boys, my boys, were joyful, superficially at least, to know they would again have a man in the house and one they seemed to like (of course what they would have rejoiced over, perhaps even dreamed it might somehow happen, was the return of their own father—but he too was on the point of remarriage). They were relieved to know their mother would be at home when they returned from school of an afternoon. They would be content to hear that all of us would be once again enjoying a more normal way of living.

Of course I am writing of what happened nineteen or twenty years ago. I don't believe it is quite the same now. More young mothers are aware, surely, of what is involved in growing up, of what their children face in the way of problems, growing pains, trauma, and so on. Gesell, Spock, Ginott, and Bettelheim are bought, even read, and perhaps digested by greater numbers of middle-class, college-educated women of today. And they know where to turn for help if the difficulties snowball beyond solution. As a matter of fact only yesterday I was talking to a bride of a few months, with an 8-year-old daughter of her own and three stepchildren belonging to her new husband. Three girls and a boy. Out of a total of six individuals, at least four of them were being treated through some form of psychiatric care.

But for me, in spite of a cultivated, if not to say intellectual upbringing in England, it quite honestly did not occur to me to worry that my children had been and were being deprived of a much needed father and that they might resent this new life bitterly. That even if they welcomed a more stable household after more than two years of female dominance, they might have some reservations. That they might, as Andrew told me when he was 27, like to do anything possible to break things up so that their real parents could get together again.

All our efforts in those early days of our marriage seemed directed to helping Andrew. And, it was true, that was more of a challenge. For *he* was the difficult child. There was no doubt about that at all. When I first saw him, he was 7 years old, with a black, wiry crew-cut and egg-shaped head. His eyes were hazel and brooding, though they could be merry too. He was a clever child, moving like quicksilver, and nervous, fidgeting or wriggling constantly, rarely at peace with himself. He was not a dreamer, then or now. His motor tendency, to use the jargon, was to continue throughout his growing up, so much so that my husband and I couldn't help but appreciate those times when he lay in bed before we put the light out, quiet, played out, with a sweetness about him and an obvious appreciation of our presence, even mine. Even more when he was recovering from illness, or exhausted after a trip. Those times his defenses were down. He seemed quite simply a little boy that we loved, and he was appealing. This didn't happen often enough.

Noah and I had planned our marriage for July. There were no orange blossoms, organ music, or proud family and friends crowding us round. We were married on a lunch hour in the dingy back streets of a town on the New Jersey side of the Hudson River. The somewhat sordid surroundings, memories of that other more innocent time, the slight but inextinguishable sense of shame, the trauma of marriage lines intoned by whomever we could find to agree to perform the ceremony, even the moment of comedy when the pastor took us aside, separately, to ask if we had read Van de Velde—this is a story best forgotten.

We had made arrangements for all three boys to be away for this summer. As I look back at it now, I feel a wrench of the heart at the very idea; Sam was so very little. But it seemed right to us then to make a complete break for them while we prepared the house in Brooklyn for its new occupants. Anyway, we told ourselves it was right.

So Andrew went back to Journey's End, the camp he had attended before, and Nick and Sam went to another one up the Hudson. Why we didn't, that first summer, put them together, I now cannot imagine. Andrew's was a better camp, less conventional and stereotyped, interesting and informal with simple unmaterialistic values. It was run by Mr. and Mrs. Allen, two rare human beings who accorded every living thing its due respect, even small boys (later on Nick and Sam did go there too, and all three loved and were loved). Second guessing like this, this Quaker camp with its small size and its farm life seems to me the perfect solution for them to get to know each other on neutral ground, with the kindness of the Allens and their counselors and the impersonal quality of non-family to bridge the chasms. If we had sent the three of them there, without of course telling them of the impending marriage beforehand, they would have had every chance to make friends with each other naturally.

As I said, we were married in July, and I said goodby to my job and old apartment without a backward glance. Unkindly, I left in the closet uptown all my unwanted rubbish—together with my unwanted memories. I moved downtown and began the preparations for receiving my new family. I was mindlessly happy, my early sense of failure lifted. Perennial optimist that I am, I just knew that everything was going to be all right. The children went off to camp and I went off also—on the arm of my new husband. I was naive, besides being self-centered. Much suffering on the part of my family might have been averted had I not been so cloud-borne when I took this second leap into the unknown.

Andrew would not be returning to his Brooklyn home. His mother had taken an apartment in Manhattan. But we were going to keep ready for him his little room over the front porch, with its three windows through which one could watch up and down the street and across at the houses opposite. When he came weekends and holidays we hoped that everything would not seem completely different or alien. For myself and my sons it was all new, all strange, but exciting too. For Andrew it was the same place, with a difference—with three differences. When he returned on weekends he would find two strange boys and a stepmother who had taken over his father, his house, his neighborhood. At least they would not have taken his room.

While the boys were away from the city during that first summer, we were happy together, Noah and I, enjoying fixing up the quarters they were to occupy, and of course getting to know each other in a more real and less tense surrounding. Somehow we had both come through the difficult period leading to separation and divorce, that no-man's-land of loneliness usually awash with a sense of guilt and failure. We entered our new marriage ardent with hope and high resolve, determined to deal lovingly and intelligently with the many fresh conundrums it was going to thrust upon us.

Now I possessed what appeared to me to be an enormous house to familiarize myself with and learn to run. It was thoroughly inconvenient in design, I came to know in time; it cost a mint to keep warm (never enough for my comfort) and was extremely hard on the legs. Its planning had included a staff of servants.

The house was fronted in gray clapboard, with large windows and a high stoop on which we were to sit with the boys during long spring and Indian summer evenings, watching strolling passers-by or playing elimination spelling games up and down the steps. It was tall and thin, vintage 1839, with nine large, high-ceilinged, gingerbread mouldinged rooms, awkwardly shallow attic, and damp, rambling basement. It had character, I admitted even then, with a certain elegance and distinction, and Andrew and Noah loved it.

I was uncertain as to my attitude, frankly. First of all, it was very big, and I was intimidated.

In it had lived the previous housekeeper—my
husband's first wife. In it had lived Andrew.
It was I, really, who was the intruder. And as
I look back on it now (at the time I never analyzed
my unease) I never really got over the sense of
being an interloper. Daphne du Maurier's
Rebecca had a lot of psychological truth to it.

And therefore I suggest to women going into
a second marriage to change the scene, to move
their new husband out of his old home, no matter
how much he objects. Either men don't have
the same sensibilities as women, or they cling
to the familiar for some kind of security against
what this unknown future might be bringing
them in the way of problems. The old ones they
know all about. Whatever *their* reason, you should
change the ambiance. You will be the better for
it, and your banished stepchild also—he will
not be returning weekends almost as a visitor, to
a familiar place filled with unfamiliar people. I
moved to my new husband's home because that
was the way he wanted it. I think this is likely
to be the attitude of many women embarking on
their second marriage; but here especially there
should be plenty of soul searching. It isn't, alas,
enough of a reason, the pleasing of a husband, and
many mistakes can occur this way.

That July we laid linoleum on the floor of

what was to be Nick and Sam's room. Before, the top floor of the house had been arranged (and rented) as an apartment with all the appurtenances, and it was our plan to have the boys eat most of their meals up in the good-sized kitchen that looked out over Brooklyn Heights rooftops. There, too, would live Mrs. White, our gentle, soft-spoken, wisely ancient, and completely wonderful housekeeper. But she came later.

In earlier days the main kitchen of the house had properly been in the large basement, with perhaps a dining room adjacent. Or else a dumbwaiter or servant carried the food and dishes up to the main floor. Now, unhappily, there was only a mini-kitchen, large enough, barely, for refrigerator, stove, and the cabinets that lined the walls. A door let out to the handkerchief-sized yard. The only counter space available, let alone a table, was a 9-inch flap on that door to the yard, and it of course had to be lowered if anyone wished to go outdoors. When we acquired a dog —well! I did not thank my predecessor who had designed a kitchen with cooking for a husband and one child only in view.

Well, we fixed everything up beautifully, we believed, and at the end of August the boys returned, the younger two to Brooklyn, the oldest to Manhattan. Of course Nick and Sam loved the endless exploring now opening up for them, even though they were a little afraid of the dark curve of the stairs down to the basement where their playroom was.

Down there also was the TV set, the laundry room, the furnace and oil storage tank. What we were most proud of were our two secret below-basement rooms. The real one, actually put to use by the underground railroad during Civil War days (this was the Heights area of Harriet Beecher Stowe and her preacher father), lay behind two concealing doors and was still filled with coal unused after conversion to oil. Actually the cannel coal in it was preferred over wood by us for use in our fireplaces, because of its marvelous crackling blaze and blue-green flames. The other underground room, more spectacular though less historic, ran under the sidewalk and street, and was large enough to house a Ping-Pong table. It was damp and no matter how strong a bulb we used in the naked overhead socket, to me it always seemed dimly lit. The Ping-Pong ball rang on the stone floor with a hollow sound. So did the boys' shouts against the vaulted ceiling. I was always chilly there. But the others loved it.

Nick and Sam lived with Noah and myself in this ancient house. Their world was on the top floor. They saw their father every other weekend when they visited him and his new family on Long Island. They seemed tolerably content and I believed they were. Andrew came weekends. He lived with his mother in Manhattan for the first five years, and went to Collegiate School. Before noon every Friday he left this historic boys' school on the West Side and took the subway to Brooklyn. He was then 9.

IV

When was I aware of being a stepmother and fully conscious of what it meant and what its implications were? The first time this really hit me came on a day in early spring, four years at least into my second marriage. It was a warm day and welcome, the first on which those banes of mothers—coats and scarves—were not really necessary. I was in the kitchen, gathering myself together to organize supper and wondering whether planning on a tuna fish salad was pushing my luck, when I heard boys' voices and simultaneously the slam of the heavy old front door. It was Andrew, home from school and accompanied, if I could believe my ears, by two-thirds at least of Grade Seven. I wiped my hands on a dish towel, quickly smoothed my hair, and went towards them (my hands were in no way wet, so this must have been a mark of my not being relaxed when Andrew came into my orbit;

I certainly never tensed up in the same way when Nick or Sam entered the house).

We were not living then in some suburban home with a well-planned kitchen designed so that Mother, working cheerily at her sink, could look up every now and then through the picture window at the front path to see if the three o'clock scholars were approaching—architectural planning providing this foreglimpse and the consequent much needed time, if she were a mother like me, to gather strength, remove her soiled apron if the children were accompanied by friends, and forcibly channel her voice and feelings into the required warm and cheerful welcome.

My kitchen looked out on a gray dust-ridden yard where only ailanthus (the Brooklyn tree) grew. It was a long way from the front door; only X-ray eyes or a periscope laid sideways could permit me to see it. Such was the layout that even boys would sometimes enter the house without my being aware of it. It was not an unusual occurrence for my husband and a guest to come in so quietly that I didn't hear and was embarrassed half to death at being caught napping on the couch with a dust cloth trailing from my hand, or with the carpet sweeper lying abandoned in the middle of the living-room floor waiting to be tripped over.

On this particular day a quick get-away from the kitchen let me take several steps into the living room before Andrew, surrounded by his friends, crowded all together through the door from the front hall. With a half-smile and a quick look up at me with his hazel eyes, he said:

"This is my . . . uh . . . stepmother, Jim, Billy, Rod. . . ." After a split second in time, long enough for the boys to shift from one foot to the other and grin in self-conscious embarrassment, they turned in unison and clattered down to the basement to play Ping-Pong.

As for me, I stood rooted where I was, paralyzed by the word I'd heard. *Stepmother*. Somehow, I'd never thought of myself as belonging under that particular label, never actually articulated the concept of a stepmother— or a stepchild, or a stepfather, if it comes to that. I suppose I'd never been really conscious of having a stepson, or being that apparently dreadful person, a stepmother. I mean deep-down conscious, for I must, like everyone else with ears to hear and eyes to read with, have been exposed to the words, but without being affected by them knowingly in any way. *Stepmother*. Suddenly I realized I didn't particularly like the sound of it. But why on earth not? What did I feel was wrong about the term? It certainly wasn't inaccurate, because I *was* Andrew's stepmother.

I sat down in my husband's favorite well-worn chair for his absent support, to try and think about the situation. I believe I had, rather carelessly, looked upon Andrew—because he was Noah's son—as a natural addition to my family, attached automatically to Noah, my new husband, but to me now as well, just another child to fit in happily with my own two. All of a sudden, as I curled up in the chair, images of Cinderella, Snow White, their stepmothers and all the other wicked stepmothers of fact and fiction, of myth and history, began to crowd into my worried head. Hadn't there been some subtle implication in Andrew's voice? He didn't like the sound of what he said, either, and it now seems clear to me that this was exactly why he had said it that way. Anyway, there was an unpleasant tone about it. I began to feel angry, until I realized how silly this was. What else could the boy have called me? He must already have used the word *stepmother* a thousand times in the course of the four years we'd been together. But there had been something in his voice just now that I hadn't noticed before. Had he not accepted me and our present rather tangled situation? I wasn't sure, myself. Nor was I sure, in this moment of sudden truth, whether I had really and truly accepted him.

But I hadn't thought about it up to this point. Noah and I had no children in common, believing, rightly or wrongly, that this would make for more and greater complications than we thought the five of us could handle or survive (being very much in love and enjoying children, obviously I always, even at that time, felt unhappy at this decision, but buried the hunger). To this we *had*, obviously, given some thought—we might well deserve reproof for following the intellect before the heart here. Interestingly enough, as I look back, the boys (Nick and Sam certainly; I don't remember clearly whether Andrew was of the same mind) had always been keen on the idea of our having a new baby. Perhaps they believed some of the tensions and strain would then roll off their backs onto another's. For most of those early years Andrew lived with his mother, coming to us from Friday afternoon after school until Monday morning. Nick and Sam, on the other hand, lived with us and visited every other weekend with their father, his new wife and growing family at their home on Long Island.

When crisis or problem struck, what did I do? Well, I'm afraid I had a way of approaching everything as it came up, on an *ad hoc* sort of basis. Problems trapped me, without warning, and so I muddled through them as best I could, hoping and struggling for some sort of viable solution—flying by the seat of my pants. My husband, when not actually part of the immediate pressure put by a specific problem, was usually able to appraise it with good sense mixed with warmth and affection. But he was terribly involved professionally in an enormous number of enterprises, with the result that I held off discussing anything with him until it had grown too much for me to handle and therefore was already a crisis, a pressure pot bursting to be solved right at that moment. And this made it hard. I don't know about him, but I, certainly, hadn't ever sat down and worked out my ideas, goals, plans, as second wife, mother to a stepson, and mother to three boys suddenly, and to them quite arbitrarily, brought together.

During those four early years of my second marriage Andrew had been young enough so that his legitimate and natural resentments had stayed below the surface. At first he wanted, quite desperately, I'm sure, to please his father, and me too. Now, it appeared, he was old enough to recognize those resentments for what they were and use them consciously when he wanted to. He had done so that afternoon. And I minded. That, of course, was the effect he had hoped to achieve, wasn't it? What, I asked myself, had

I done wrong? Where had I left the trolley track, if I had? Perhaps this was all very natural, a move towards maturity on my part as a stepmother and his as a stepson and an adolescent to boot. But what role, actually, did I want to follow, what exactly was my ideal here? I wondered, in this orgy of self-pity and self-inquisition, just how close I came, or how far off I was from the picture I wanted to present to Andrew. Or was it the picture to my husband that mattered to me? Did I care most about the image *he* would have of me as a *good* and not a *wicked* stepmother?

    I looked around our living room. The chairs and sofa were definitely on the dilapidated side, but how could it be otherwise with three growing boys, a dog, and a kitten who loved to scratch and who couldn't see any connection between a store-bought scratching post and his claws. But the chairs were comfortable and well sat in, and I regarded them with affection. Books lined the walls from floor to ceiling, and in my mind's eye I could see the flickering flames of a winter fire in the empty old grate and feel its warmth and that of the surrounding room. How could there be unhappiness or antagonism here? Yet clearly there was—perhaps a good deal. And as I probed my own feelings, heretofore hidden and pushed below many layers of cognizance, I could remember and acknowledge my own periodic despair and resentment because of Andrew's highly difficult behavior and Noah's consequent anger at him, his own sense of guilt more often than not taken out on me. Nick and Sam must have felt bewildered, perhaps a bit desolate, as the drama of the family's life swirled around others; because they were quieter and calmer, less belligerent and intent on stirring up the dust, they were more in the background.

I don't think there was anything so out of the ordinary in all this, in Andrew's or my feelings, or those of the others. The question was, did it have to be that way? Could any of the bad moments have been avoided? My answer is yes, I think some at the very least can be softened if not completely eliminated. That is why I am writing this book.

I made many mistakes. Millions of them, I suppose. Some of them, I am now convinced, need not have occurred had I done even a modicum of planning at the time of my second marriage, or even better, shortly before it took place. If only I had done some studying as well as planning, a little reading up on what the pitfalls might be, so that I could be aware of them before I fell in, so that I could learn of what others had encountered and where they too had erred or had succeeded.

Part of my professional life had been spent in research; I had been a *Time* researcher, had worked for the OWI during the war, and for British Information Services. Clearly it was just plain stupidity not to apply some of whatever skill I had learned to my own life. I could have found out what were the classic problems inherent in a second marriage, what were the special moments and points of stress. If I had done some homework, there is little doubt in my own mind that I would have been the gainer. But chiefly, I should have accepted the fact that I was not Andrew's mother and never could be. I could never feel towards him the way his mother did; and he could never feel towards me as a son. The relationship is a different one—an even more difficult one—and I think it can only be successful if this is understood. If I had done so, I would not only have been a better stepmother to Andrew, but a better mother to Nick and Sam and a better wife to Noah.

Marshaling my thoughts into some sort of order as I sat alone in the living room, I began at the beginning. What exactly was a *stepchild?* Right there, in the middle of the carpeted floor,

I spread out the huge Webster Unabridged, and Volume X, "sole-Sz" of the great Oxford Dictionary. It was a fine starting place, because immediately I discovered something I had not known. I would have guessed that the word was connected in some way with a "step"—up or down depending on your point of view—and meaning removed from the real, or direct relationship. Not so. According to Webster, the "step" in stepchild is from the Anglo-Saxon word "stoep," meaning "to be deprived." Out of Anglian fens and marshes came the word now a synonym for cruelty and indifference when prefixed to *mother*. Webster continued: ". . . to bereave, as children of their parents. A combining form denoting a relative by virtue of a remarriage, especially the remarriage of a parent."

    I turned to the dark blue dignity of the Oxford English Dictionary. It put the derivation from the Anglo-Saxon in this way: ". . . prefixed to terms of relationship (as father, son, brother) to form designations for the degrees of affinity resulting from the remarriage of a widowed parent." Obviously Mr. Webster acknowledged at least by implication the possibility of divorce, while on the other side of the Atlantic nothing but the widowhood of one parent can lead to the remarriage of the other. The important point seems to be in both of these definitions the blood relationship existing between child and one parent who remarries and thus introduces the step-relationship into the family.

 I found myself considerably confused over the terms *stepchild, foster child,* and *adopted child* —all meaning different things. I realized then they are frequently and wrongly used interchangeably. For I looked them up, too. A foster parent "performs the duties," says Webster, "of a parent to the child of another by rearing the child as his own." An adopted child is one taken voluntarily into a relationship, become as if one's own. There is today a legal connotation to the term "adopted child," whereas a foster child is, at the behest of parent or court, returnable to the real, blood parent. We must agree that there is a great difference emotionally between the position of a stepchild and that of an adopted, or a foster child. The parents of the latter know what they are. And one of them is *not* replacing the real parent. Jealousy, and resentment too, have no place. (Only recently a divorced friend of mine came up to me, excitedly waving a clipping from *The New York Times.* "The courts have made a new ruling," he shouted in my ear. "Now I can take Jimmy as a dependent, even though he's my stepson. What do you think of that!"

"How come," I questioned "No qualifications or anything?"

My friend put spectacles on nose, and read from the clip: "The Superior Court ruled today that foster children. . . ."

"Hey, stop, stop right there," I interrupted. "Jimmy's not your foster child. That ruling has nothing to do with you."

"He's my stepson. Stepson, foster son, what's the difference?"

My friend descended to earth with a bump as I explained the semantic and legal differences of child-parent relationships.)

But back to my researches of many years ago. I was, to be sure, able to find out the definitions of the words. But little about other people or other children in our situation. There were plenty of statistics published by the government, by insurance companies and other organizations, as to the number of children and orphans in our nation, but nowhere could I find any figures on the numbers of stepchildren.

What is absolutely sure is this: there are literally thousands who sit in the same boat as I did when I remarried, who also are fumbling ineptly at the oars in an attempt to blunder on towards family cohesion and happiness.

There are no official figures, only estimates, on

the total number of minor children in the United States who have lived through the divorce of their parents. Nor, of course, is it known how many of these children have become stepchildren because of the remarriage of a parent. In 1954, four years after my remarriage, an attempt was made for the first time at extracting from census data the number of children who in that year became "children of divorce." The count was 341,000, but it is hard to evaluate this figure, because there was no information on how many stepchildren were in the population before. That year the total child population (under 18) was roughly 53,900,000.

In 1961, when the number of children under 18 had snowballed to about 66,000,000, attention was at last turned to the problems of the stepchild, by Anne W. Simon, in her book *Stepchild in the Family* (published in 1964). The demographer Paul Jacobson (author of *American Marriage and Divorce*) made a special statistical study for her book and arrived at the figure of stepchildren under 18 in the U.S. for 1961 to be 7 million.

Each year the number grows. There were 701,000 children of parents divorced in 1967, the latest full year for which figures are available (as this book is being written). In the nine month period from January to September, 1968, there was a 10% increase in divorce decrees granted, over the same period in 1967.

At last the U.S. Census Bureau is acknowledging the social importance of accurate data on the number of our stepchildren. But it is too late to obtain statistics on them through the 1970 Census. Assuming only the same rate of increase that prevailed up to 1961, the 1970 total may well reach the staggering figure of 12 million or more. In the 1980 census there will most likely be a question on the number of stepchildren in each household. When that total is officially announced, a new awareness of the magnitude of the stepchild-stepparent problem may be expected.

The marital conflicts between unhappy adults (eventually leading to divorce) can have a far more demoralizing effect on their children and result in far greater bewilderment, misery, and trauma, than actual separation and divorce itself. If men and women who are contemplating remarriage understand this and try to compensate for the past by reknitting and mending, by forming an untense even if new family unit, they will go far towards "normalizing" their children once again. No, *normalizing* isn't the word. They will help their children *accept* the new situation, and get the most out of it, instead of fighting it and hoping to destroy it—or destroy themselves by never letting up on their yearning for a past that will not return.

Perhaps there are women who, left alone with children through death or divorce, are able to temper their wonder, their euphoria, at the miracle of a second chance at love and marriage —women who are able to weigh the necesary pros and cons before a second try at matrimony, who marry again only after careful planning that includes the children and their welfare.

I am not addressing myself to those well-organized, thoughtful, and intelligent people who have sifted through all the problems to come. Because of this premarital exercise of mental effort, they will have proved more successful than I in welding together the members of what was two separate groups into a single, harmonious family unit. Nor do I speak to those in this world—and I am privileged to know some of them—who are able to make happy all those they touch, who turn all relationships to gold, who take all difficulties in their stride, and who thus are not insecure, often at a loss, resenting, or resented.

This book is not for them, but for those like myself who do not have this magic touch and who must make a conscious effort to think to a far greater degree of the others involved. This does not necessarily mean that if I had been more thoughtful, less selfishly inclined, it would have been better for all concerned if I had not remarried. I do not think this to be the case— although after reading my oldest son's view of those early years I cannot be sure. It is how it was done and how approached that I am concerned with, as contrasted with how it might have been done, so that less hurt would have been caused and fewer people damaged. Children are hurt so easily— by a careless action, a loose word, seeming indifference (caused perhaps only by fatigue), a brusque gesture, a sharp look, or a kiss neglected. If we try hard enough, most of us can remember a phrase tossed off by an unthinking adult during our own growing up that bitterly wounded us, to the point of sticking in our memory. My mother, over 40 when I was born, said to me once: "We *are* good friends, aren't we! It's as though I'm your grandmother." At 10, this didn't have a great impact; I may even have been pleased. But as the years progressed, the comment packed an ever increasing wallop that spelled "uninvolvement." Cannot we ourselves avoid inflicting this kind of wound?

    Nor is this book for parents, of either sex, who care so little about their own children that, because of concomitant problems in the divorce situation, they reject them completely (I know several children who, living with one parent, have never been held in the absent parent's arms since the divorce). Or for those who are not troubled by the unhappiness of a stepchild, who like Cinderella's stepmother, favor their own and get away with what cruelties they can towards the others. These parents use their children as tools for the purpose of hurting a previous mate (many of us find ourselves doing this, but to most of us the discovery is a bitter one, and we try to avoid it in the future). One recently divorced woman of my acquaintance is recovering, happily, from a heart attack. Her 20-year-old daughter, living in Oregon with the father at present, visited her in the hospital after a voyage of three thousand miles. The mother was delighted to see her child —until she was presented with a paper from the ex-husband. It was a legal document for her to sign, deeding to him her property in the event of her death. No, this book is not for such readers as these.

 Some time ago I came across the opinion of a psychiatrist, one widely quoted in material about unhappy children and their divorced parents. It reads: "The children of divorced parents are insecure; whatever their appearance, you will find somewhere a panicky loss of morale, a figurative hanging of the head." Clearly far more affection is needed even than one might imagine, a more frequent hug given as you meet your stepchild and your own children too, a greater understanding of resentments, and more flexibility on all sides and in all quarters. I am now aware, but I wasn't when I remarried, that Andrew and the other boys were operating under a great handicap. Whether they felt it consciously or not, their position in society was far from a normal one. Even living as we did in New York City, where the incidence of divorce and remarriage and children involved is possibly higher than in any other location in the country, this was the case. So it was this knowledge, sensed in some way, that put the special note in Andrew's voice when he introduced his friends to me. And their embarrassment was not only the natural self-consciousness of children towards an adult, but also their reaction to the uncomfortable fairy-tale-associated word—*stepmother*.

V

"I don't like string beans or peas, and I don't want any bread and butter!" Andrew couldn't have sounded more emphatic if he'd banged his fist on the glass-topped table at which we both sat, like adversaries, facing one another. Even at 10, the boy was forceful.

"Come on, Andy, have some vegetables, do." I tried to stare him down, but I kept my voice calm and gentle—I hoped.

"I don't like vegetables. I want more chicken wings." We glared at each other, and his dark eyes were sullen. I pushed the dish of string beans in his direction, holding firmly, if nervously, to my principles: a balanced meal consisted of some meat, some vegetables, some potatoes, a piece of fruit, and a glass of milk; if still hungry, fill up on bread and butter and a second glass of milk. That's how I'd been brought up, and it still made sense to me.

Andrew just tilted his chair back, saying

nothing. Those dents in the rubber tile floor are increasing by leaps and bounds, I thought abstractedly.

"One can't just eat what one wants," I said finally. It sounded feeble. Why *can't* one pick and choose, children as well as adults, who do just that, notably Andrew's father—his prime example. I hurried on before the boy had time to come out with the unanswerable: "Dad does." Or: "I always have"; or, worst of all, "My *mother* lets me."

"It isn't healthy, and besides, it costs too much, or it would if we all behaved like that. When you're one of a family of five, things are different." I wasn't convincing even to myself, and perhaps that last had not been the most tactful remark I could have made. But I *was* the cook, and still stronger than he was, this 10-year-old stepson of mine.

It was Friday lunch, and Andrew, whose school let out at noon, was alone with me and at my mercy (it seemed to me the other way around). Mrs. White, our gentle housekeeper, was out shopping, and Nick and Sam ate at their schools. The full-length window of the dining alcove looked out on our bleak sooty little yard. It hardly seemed tempting enough to appeal to Andrew, as he perched on the edge of his wrought iron chair, rocking it back and forth, mouth set and brows creased. This lunch table exchange was typical of what happened when Andrew ate in the Brooklyn house and stemmed from one of our basic conflicts. He thought less than nothing of routine or rules, except how to beat the game. I believed firmly in them as a basis for family living. And that was one of the troubles, right there. Andrew thought, acted, and breathed as an individual, a headstrong and willful individual. I worked for the unit as a whole (I told myself) and believed in bromidic things like sportsmanship, self-control, responsibility. On this particular occasion, I saw I couldn't win and so I left the lists.

Andrew didn't win, either. There *were* no more chicken wings. He may well have been still hungry. He certainly ate none of my vegetables. A far cry from *my* schooldays, when food left on my plate was returned to be eaten at the next meal!

Of course, one can and should forget the rules sometimes. But as a rationale for living, they made sense to me, and as a pattern for a family, I thought them a must. Or was I clinging to them a bit desperately—the raft on which I survived or sank?

Although born in the United States (Ticonderoga, New York,—apple-pie American), I had spent my childhood and adolescence in England, where my father was an Oxford don. Because my mother too was an intellectual (a feminist and Fabian, it might be said, in the days of the Webbs, Russells, Coles, the Bloomsbury circle, suffragettes, the railroad strike), a writer and translator, and so busy, my sisters and I had nannies and then a governess before the years spent in boarding schools (this sounds moneyed— it wasn't, not on a professor's salary in those days; I believe my parents borrowed from American relatives for our education). Our lives were regulated. As I look back on it, the routine, though often irritating and impersonalized (herein perhaps lies one of its strengths), must have been a source of calm in the house and security to its inmates. Adhered to, taken for granted, it also meant that my mother didn't have squabbles with us about the trivial matters of daily life. She could be above the teacup storms and was. Perhaps the fact that my mother had no sons played some role in the benign state of affairs. Whatever my attitude towards the British nanny and boarding school syndrome was at the time (because later I was to realize my parents neglected us quite a bit), I was no battler against *routine*, and in fact I had put this pattern into practice rather positively during the organizing of my life during my first marriage. Naturally, I carried it over into the second, and therefore there was no change of philosophy, really, for Nick and Sam.

For Andrew, it was different. And how different! Son of a brilliant, autocratic father and stylish, attractive, sophisticated mother, he had been permitted to be anarchic from the time he'd first tottered on two feet. His parents' attitudes and practices were chaotic, by my lights, but by the same token exciting and stimulating, particularly so to a small boy. Their son, lively and personable, lovable when in a good mood, was their only child and very much part of their lives. When he was a nuisance they might ignore him or bat him down. Neither of them believed in the "children should be seen and not heard" theory on which I had been raised, and which I, somewhat subscribing to, had used in the raising of my own two boys. This isn't to say that no parental edicts or ukases were uttered by Andrew's father and mother. Of course there were, plenty of them. But not always the same ones as mine, and certainly not so routinely that they could be taken as a matter of course and thus relegated to their proper place, accepted without fuss or insistence.

So I was faced with a dilemma—one most likely confronting all women who enter into a second marriage with children of both partners. Did I change my own rules, thereby having to teach my own children to accept a different viewpoint after they had come to understand and abide by my previous precepts, and thus confuse them and myself and undermine my own self-confidence to boot? Or did I, with as much kindness and patience as I could muster, and as little rigidity as possible, influence my stepchild so that *he* would be the one to learn to fit in? I chose the latter course, not because I systematically laid out my choices in front of me and made my selection as I am doing now, but by instinct.

Andrew had no truck with my concept of an orderly world. English nursery tenets were as foreign to him as their country of origin. Mention of them by me met with open contempt and disregard—usually also with a snort of derision. It soon got so that I didn't "bring up" Nick and Sam in front of Andrew, for fear that his rebellion would spread and that I would have a mutiny aboard my ship on the part of all hands instead of just one. Also, I must admit, for fear of his hostility and possible mockery as well.

I tried to make nonconformity more palatable by describing my own shortcomings as a child, and the boys were amused at my stories of shoving my unwanted food—mashed potatoes in particular, I remember—under the carpet, so that it wouldn't be dished up for me again, cold and congealed, at supper time. Of course, after that, they would remind me of it with considerable glee. It would be lovely if I could say I tried with loving kindness and tender loving care to win Andrew over to the habits accepted by the majority—and not only him but his father as well, for Noah was almost as rebellious, and hooted almost as often as his son did over my hoped-for nursery manners. It wasn't like that at all. I just went ahead with what I felt and believed in my heart, bones, and fingertips was right and good for me, the boys, and my husband—as a family. When it didn't work, I cried. I cried rather a lot, and I didn't have the mother wit to use tears as a weapon, either. They were tears of frustration, over which I had little control, and they lost their effectiveness with their frequency. In middle age, alas, I have learned some wisdom, at least. I know now that people differ, that what is right for one is not necessarily right for another (and I don't cry as much!).

I also know now that the enforced merging and compromising (for of course all of us made thousands of compromises—we were forced to) of two ways of looking at things may benefit everyone, but only in the long run. In the short hundred yard dash, it hurts. In fact, to mix my sports metaphors, it feels to the wife and mother in the center position rather like a football scrimmage must to a player long out of training.

I would advise the new stepmother to follow the course I took and not alter her own life style for one important reason—not because my rules or behavior or attitudes were necessarily the right ones, even for me. But because she must believe in herself, know who she is, and be at peace with herself. The stepmother's self-confidence and lack of doubts or wavering over what she thinks to be right or wrong can be crucial in giving the individuals of her new and enlarged family the emotional boost and stability they need to succeed in the complex new skein of relationship into which they've been tossed. If she falls to pieces, wavers even more than customary over the right path to follow because it is one uncharacteristic for her, things are likely to come unraveled. I know of more than one stepmother (including myself) who went through a hell of allergic itching before deciding to follow her *own* instincts and set of values.

Just how easy her job will be inevitably depends largely on her stepchild's father—on his tolerance and good sense when he too is faced with other habits and other mores. Like his child, he too must learn to fit and to conform, and he too may find his resentment, his impatience, his irritation over what is new and what seems vastly unimportant, very hard to curb. His talent or lack of it for yielding gracefully to his new wife and what she believes to be right and wrong can make the difference between smooth seas or stormy ones. I am not advocating here a mother-ruled roost. Far from it, for I am a firm believer in father's wearing the pants—but not in dealing with day-to-day trivia. However, of course, even on this level the mother is not always right—her own ideas and rules she wishes the family to follow are sometimes ridiculous. If her husband is able to point this out with good humor and affection, not showing her up, so to speak, in front of the joint brood before them, her troubles will be enormously lessened.

    Naturally, I didn't find any of this easy or smooth going. I tensed up far too often under the strain of achieving balance and stability in dealing with what was once two separate groups. I was self-conscious with Noah over the children, and my innocent and happy games played with my sons yesterday seemed today like a maleless heaven without stress or conflict. But there wasn't really nearly as strong a sense of battle lines drawn and held to as the reader might imagine from my description.

So, I established habits and a routine—or at least made the attempt: breakfast at a certain time, the children taken or sent off to school, Noah dispatched to the office, housework, marketing, cooking, all done—homework overseen, play and bedtime story hour, followed by the peace and surcease of "parent hour," when Noah and I could, if not too exhausted, drop into our chairs and relax, and enjoy each other as we had when we were "courting."

It was quite a strain. The easy way of dealing with children and with the problems that normally come up between members of the same family who have grown up together was not there—at least not in the early years. I felt awkward as I tried to manage this strange and enormous house, struggling to fit my two small boys as smoothly as possible into Noah's old habits, while easing *his* adapting to a new wife and two-boy routine with which he was totally unfamiliar. In trying to build a solid framework for this new family I often seemed silly, even to myself, and I became rather self-conscious when I tried to insist on certain rules. The most minor and stupid things led too often to cross words, shouts, imagined slights, and tears.

As an example of the trivial sort of thing that can cause disruption in the stepfamily, let me describe our dental situation. We—me, but Nick and Sam in particular—had far more of a problem with our teeth than Andrew or his parents (this in itself was cause for some unconscious disdain by Andrew and Noah). Orthodonture for the younger boys was a must, and was accepted by them. They even liked the dentist and did not dread visits to him. (Partly, perhaps, because he was an extraordinary individual, who, when I was separated and living alone, exaggerated his editing and rewrite needs on articles, or speeches for delivery before dental societies, to help me pay "in kind" for his work on our teeth.) When he bade them brush their teeth "up and down" instead of across, they believed he knew what he was talking about and tried to do what he asked. I passed this stricture on to Noah, so that he could encourage them also, and perhaps give Andrew the same advice. But he pooh-poohed the whole bit, and made fun of me and them as well. I despaired. Parents with children in common are, I think, more likely to accept this sort of thing without a thought or a word—certainly without exerting any sort of disruptive influence. And now, many many years later, Noah brushes his teeth up and down. I wonder why?

When the stepchild lives permanently with his stepmother and father, the kind of pattern I was after can be established rapidly enough, so that the deeper necessities of love, affection, respect—the really important elements—can be worked on. But if he comes, like Andrew, only on weekends, it will take longer and be more difficult. When you put together two sets of children, brought up by totally different rules of behavior in very different frameworks—bewilderment, tensions, and troubles are bound to result, and not just on the children's part either, but for grownups as well. It must have been extremely hard for Andrew to be confronted with such differing attitudes about almost everything in his day-to-day life; how could I have expected him to act as though he enjoyed it all?

Sam has told me recently that what he found most difficult to handle when *he* went on weekends to visit *his* father and *his* stepmother, was the fact that they were less strict than I was, that the children were not bound by the rules of behavior I had instilled in him. For years, he said, this upset him profoundly—until he discovered that this had not stopped them from growing into a family welded together by respect and affection. He learned that being *different* did not make something, or someone, "worse."

For the first three years of our marriage, Andrew came to our house weekends and holidays.

Crew cut abristle, and pennywhistle bright, he brought immediate change to our household, a zip to the atmosphere and a sense of excitement among everyone in the house. It was all-pervasive, his influence (if influence is not too strong a word for a 10-year-old?). Life was never dull with Andrew around. But it could be uncomfortable, and the supercharged air sometimes caused tension rather than joyousness. Andrew had to be interested in the game that was projected, in the book, in the play, or in the record or TV program. If not, his boredom or distaste was all too clear, and at the least, enjoyment for others was lessened. At the most, because the boys wanted his participation, the game or book was changed if he wasn't interested. He was *the* cog in everything that went on while he was in the house; and he influenced everything—for good and bad both. I know now, and I use today's vocabulary, that I was always uptight when he was around. Perhaps I still am. Maybe he is as well. The difference today is that either of us can leave if we are too uncomfortable!

The close and fine relationship between Noah and Andrew could, on occasion, make for trouble because there was present this quality of intensity and immediacy—very different from that to which I and my sons had been accustomed. I was more casual with them, and I did not give them constant demonstrations of my love for them. I didn't feel it to be necessary. Above all, I treated them as children. With Andrew it was different (is it becoming a refrain, "with Andrew it was different"?). His parents had naturally been more absorbed in him as an only child than they would or could be if he had had siblings. At the time, I considered him to be overstimulated, needing excitement, movement, food for body and brain constantly, exposed at too early an age to adult pleasures and pastimes. But the sum of it was that the boy had no doubt in the world that his parents loved him very much, and that everything that happened to him and everything that he did was of interest to them.

So the different parents of the three boys in our household held attitudes and beliefs that were not alike. Of course this made for trouble. Because Noah was not the father of Nick and Sam, his absorption and interest in them was far less and in a lower key. The chemistry was just not there, no matter how much he tried to tell me and himself that he loved all three of them equally. It didn't reach his guts in the same way—and this was plain. Nor did he feel any guilt over them, as he did with his son and his disruption of the boy's life. It was something he was never able to forget, and he tells me today this guilt was the reason he was so concentrated in his attentions towards Andrew on those weekend days.

This might have been clear to me from the beginning, for a certain incident pointed up the difference in relationship between Noah and his son Andrew, and his stepsons Nick and Sam. When we were married, Noah had told me very seriously about his periods of gloom and how he might return from the office in the evening silent and unapproachable, withdrawn for a while. I wasn't to mind, he said, for it had nothing to do with me. I tried to school myself not to pay attention or take it personally, to hold myself back and to chatter about inconsequentials that did not call for response. It was hard.

How much harder for a small boy, who hadn't had a man around for a long time, thick brown hair tousled and prune eyes eager and welcoming, full of ebullience and joyful that the man of the house was coming in the front door. For the first few days after his return from camp that summer to life in the new house, Nick would tear down the stairs and throw himself at Noah's legs, hugging him and yearning for response. Noah couldn't give it.

"Your face is dirty," he'd say. And before the boy had retreated up the stairs again and was completely out of earshot he'd say to me: "Can't you keep the boys upstairs when I come home, so that the house is quiet for a bit?"

And he asked me to stop Nick from greeting him in this fashion every night. "They can come down later, when I've got my breath," he told me. It was a heartbreaking task. I carried it out because, I told myself, there was always the possibility that consequent antagonism and the showing of it on Noah's part might be worse. But now I wonder—maybe Noah would have been the one to get over his need for shaking off the world and its problems when he entered his home at night, and perhaps this would have been the better result, rather than the rejection of a small boy's overt affection.

On a conscious level (and subconscious too) I don't think my boys were bothered too much by Noah's differing attitudes to them than to Andrew, of whom they were fond. It did trouble me. I wanted so much for them all to be treated the same, to feel equally loved, equally important in the eyes of the two grown-ups they lived with. I wanted the same for each boy. But I wanted the impossible. Noah's treatment of them was much more in tune with his real feelings, while I lived in a romantic dream.

Children must be treated alike—objectively.

But it is important for the new family to realize and understand that the attitude of a stepfather to his stepchildren, of a stepmother to hers, *is* different from his attitude to his own children and her attitude to hers. It cannot help but be. We, as stepparents, do not wish to make any difference in our minds, but it is there just the same, and the sooner we accept it the healthier will be the climate of the home. This is quite apart from the obvious truth that children are not alike, that they have different talents, abilities, tastes, and so realistically are treated differently anyway. In our situation, Noah was sure there was equality all along the line. But it existed in words only. He would repeat to me that he loved Nick and Sam, that Andrew loved me, as well as Nick and Sam, and when his son kissed him goodnight he would bid the boy come over to me to do the same. Andrew and I were both a bit uncomfortable as we did what he asked. Probably it is best to let such demonstrations develop naturally, or not take place at all. Noah's words didn't make the reality come true. Love in the stepfamily comes, if ever, with time and shared experiences. Giving it a boost with a hug and a kiss on the part of adults can't hurt, either, but *spontaneously,* not on order.

Noah was aware of the perils in the temptation to make every weekend seem like Christmas in the way of gifts, and a birthday in the way of excitement. He saw that he had to fight against this for Andrew's sake, and his own, and that of the rest of us; for this would only emphasize the transitory nature of Andrew's visits and set him apart from the other boys. Underneath the superficial enjoyment of being the focus of attention, there must lie, it seems to me, a frustrated feeling of being a guest, even an intruder, in the house. The ideal background for the weekend child is a sense from adults and children alike that it is only a short time since he was here—let's fill him in on what's happened and go on very naturally accepting him as a vital cog in the machine—which is nevertheless geared to his absence on weekdays and takes this absence for granted.

With us, it always seemed to be *next* weekend that was going to work out so ideally. *This* one is coming apart at the seams, with hostility, emotion, overstimulation, hopes keyed up and then let down. As for me, I dreaded the weekends. I found that I was constantly feeling hurt (seeing Nick and Sam left out, or believing that they were).

The stepmother is bound to feel hurt, unless she is a most unusually generous and unneurotic person. When her husband is concentrating on his visiting son or daughter, a gesture—no matter how friendly—that indicates her wish to join in and be a part of the fun may be treated by them both as an intrusion, even though they more than likely have no intent to hurt her at all. It *is* an intrusion. They will probably include any other child as a matter of course, but the spotlight will nevertheless be on the father's child who has come to visit. So that I, seeing this, felt that Nick and Sam were being either left out or treated like second-class citizens. It took me forever to see that my attempts or fumbles to make Noah and Andrew understand this and change only made matters worse.

Children, even one's own, are hardy little animals. Mine would vastly have preferred to play with their stepfather, in an unusually involved and playful mood, and his son, their stepbrother, than be protected by me even if they *were* on the periphery of the circle of activity. Of course, father and son should learn to accept stepbrothers, even stepmother, and share their joys and ploys. Easier said than done. The most important thing on Noah's mind those weekends when Andrew came was Andrew—not me, or Nick, or Sam. I felt excluded and hurt, and on behalf of my two sons as well. The weekends were frequently unhappy, in spite of the baseball games in a nearby lot, the walks along the mysterious, deserted, shadow-filled docks and piers of the Brooklyn waterfront, in spite of the "famous" hot dogs and marshmallows toasted over the fire, and charades afterwards. Weekends meant trouble, fights, excitement, maybe tears—and it meant homework to be completed for Monday's school.

For my cousin Maud, stepmother of two daughters, weekends meant something else again. "When they come into the house Friday afternoon, I become the servant of the place," she told me on one of many occasions she came to me for comfort and a sympathetic ear. " '*Our* mother doesn't make *us* wash dishes when we're tired, or make our beds,' they tell me when I try to get them to help. They throw her at me all the time, poor woman, so that I can't stand the sound of her name, or even the thought of her. '*She* knows how to cook,' they say, the clear implication being that *I* don't; *she* makes them *groovey* clothes, has good taste when she buys them a gift. Oh Lord, it's the end, Pat. Sometimes I feel I can't go on any longer."

"How about Norm, doesn't *he* make them pitch in?" I asked, remembering Noah's perhaps too stern attitude towards Andrew over this sort of thing.

"Norm?" There was real bitterness in Maud's voice as she uttered the name of her husband, whom I knew full well she was crazy about. "When they defy me and I expect him to intervene, he gives me that look, *you* know, that says: 'Please, don't force the issue.' *Of course* he doesn't want his short time with them spoiled by bickering, I know that. It's actually more trouble than it's worth, for both of us, because the atmosphere is thicker than pea soup with their sulks, if I cross them in any way. Pam and Penny, they call the tune, and Norman dances. Me, I sit in the corner and feel sorrier and sorrier for myself. Penny flirts with him so outrageously that I'm jealous of my own stepdaughter. And Pam! Now she's older she knows just exactly how to hurt Norm, how to use him against me. And she gives or withholds her affections. Even her very presence. You know, Pat, now she won't come at all if during the week he hasn't agreed to give her something she asks for."

Maud's tone of venom, and the tears soaking into my green sweater as I hugged her, made me realize my own good fortune regarding the simple nature of *my* problems.

The most important thing a stepmother can develop, or at least one of the most important things, is a tough skin, and the ability to avoid being sorry for herself. Today I am ashamed of the amount of self-pity I wallowed in. It surely did *me* no good, only harm, and the rest of the family as well.

As I think of the weekend homework, I remember Andrew lying sprawled on the living-room floor over a textbook. This brings me to the question of respect. The building up of mutual respect is a very important matter in the early days of the step-relationship. This applies, I believe, whether you have stepdaughters or stepsons, whether you are a stepmother or a stepfather. It is a vital factor in any sort of human relationship, and doubly so when this relationship is as brimful of problems as the one we are concerned with.

There are ways for a stepparent to achieve this respect, even on the part of an unruly, hostile boy between 9 and 13—as Andrew was during this period. Because a wife loves her new husband, it does not automatically follow that she will love his child. It is in fact pretty unlikely that she will, no matter how much or how ardently she wishes to do so. Nor will he love her—no matter how often his father tells him to kiss her goodnight, as Noah did, or tells him that he surely loves his stepmother because his father does (this is only wasted energy and can obviously have the reverse effect). Love, unlike spontaneous combustion, does not occur very often between children and adults in a matter of minutes, with a look, a word, or even a hug. There are certain very natural but powerful feelings between children and stepparents that most of us don't own up to, even in our secret hearts. We refuse to admit to dislike, fear, distrust or, if the *dramatis personae* are older, to the emotional or sexual love that can develop. These are "bad," so we must not recognize them. If we were able to, it might make for a more honest atmosphere and make easier, I think, the process of ironing out the differences and problems that are bound to be present.

Sooner or later, and usually sooner, the stepchild is going to resent his new stepmother, and she will probably resent him. My advice is, accept it, and don't feel guilty at your periodic lack of pleasant feelings towards him (keep it to yourself, though, and don't discuss it with your husband). What the stepmother can most profitably do is work towards winning the respect and affection of her stepchild. It takes patience, but the chances are that with success, the feeling will become mutual.

It is not so easy for a child to find ways to win his stepparent's respect; adults must provide opportunities for this. Expect your stepson to do the right thing, to behave, to do his best with his studies, to be a help with younger children. Show him you value him, trust him, and respect his ideas and opinions. Even if he lets you down—and he will—or cannot deliver on four occasions, maybe he will on the fifth. Give him the chance to try.

How can the stepmother gain her young stepson's respect? First of all, by her attitude. If she can be unhurried with him, interested, fair, gentle, and reasonably intelligent, he will learn to count on her for certain things, to know how she will act in given situations. It is important for him to know, for instance, what she expects of him, or that when he does something she will not approve of, she will punish him (he may, at that moment, be wanting, even asking, for the punishment to be meted out to him). He needs to know that she will not go to his father with accounts of his misdeeds; even if his initial feeling to her is one of open antagonism, there will be respect, however grudging, if he can trust her word and her discretion.

He will begin to respect and even like her, perhaps, if his stepmother is able to help with his homework, without making him feel too stupid in the process; if she can throw a ball hard, or tell a good and scary ghost story. Most important of all, if she commands the respect of his father.

If it becomes impossible for him to be pleasant,

and a pattern of misbehavior sets in (which it does all too easily), then it is all the more important for the adults to look to him to be good, to expect it, and not show him they fear the opposite. It can be fatal if the negative aspects of every situation are emphasized (this, unhappily, is what *we* did): how can we stop him from being naughty; or what shall we do if he doesn't behave? Steady encouragement to do right must surely pay off in the end. Andrew's father, himself an only child, was also in trouble much of his childhood and saw some sort of echo in Andrew's behavior. Perhaps this is why he accepted it more easily than I, and also why, in a way, he had less patience with him. He was less emotional, however.

    A child will be affected in different ways according to the reasons for his parents' separation. If his mother has died, the stepmother will in some respects have a rougher time of it, for the blood mother's image will naturally become idealized as it dims, and she, the substitute, will suffer forever by the comparison. However, I cannot see that this matters very much. His mother will be in a separate compartment. Once the child is over the sharpness of the immediate loss, he will not be emotionally and continually torn by the existence of two homes, where his father and mother live, apart. And it will be very much to his own interest to get along with his stepmother and to fit her as best he can into the place once held by his mother.

If his mother is alive, on the other hand, the child may be very confused as to the role of his father's new wife. What is she doing there beside his father? Why does his father like her? It is very possible that the child will believe that any turning towards her on his part or any growing feeling of affection will be disloyal to his natural mother. What may result is not only a disturbing sense of guilt towards his absent mother, but also a belief that overt acts of antagonism to his stepmother show his loyalty to his own mother and are therefore justified. This loyalty can be very intense.

Andrew was rent by it. One Friday evening he was sitting at the big desk in the library, doing his homework. He was unusually quiet and absorbed, working away with his pencil only briefly between long intervals of chewing on it.

"What are you doing?" his father asked.

"I've a theme to hand in Monday," Andrew replied without lifting his head.

"What's the subject?" Noah persisted.

"Mr. Hodge said we could choose our own," said Andrew, looking up at last. "Mine is Robert E. Lee."

"He was quite a man," Noah said slowly. "Why him, though? How about Abe Lincoln, or Stonewall Jackson?"

I remember how seriously Andrew replied.

"You see, Dad," he explained, "General Lee loved his state of Virginia. He also loved his country. It was like me, with you in Brooklyn and Mother in New York. Lee had to choose. It was hard."

"I see," said Noah thoughtfully as Andrew bent his head to the paper in front of him.

It was a poignant moment. And it was true; any criticism of his mother by his father (not that it happened very often, for Noah tried to be careful) usually called forth a display of strong and antagonistic feelings on Andrew's part towards his father. Even today this is so.

I think the crux of the stepmother's job is to convince her stepson that she is *not* trying to take his mother's place. If she succeeds, he will not feel guilty if he likes her. And for her part perhaps if she is able to regard herself as an older sister, or a camp counselor, *she* will feel less hurt when her opinion is not asked, or when she is not made welcome at a game of catch in the yard.

One of the clearest roads to a calm household is the avoidance of setting up situations or occasions when your stepchild, acting perfectly naturally, is bound to irritate you by his behavior—as for example taking him to visit *your* relatives, whom he has never seen or heard of before and about whom he couldn't care less.

How to gain a stepchild's respect? Find ways. Story reading, story telling, reciting poems, singing—but be empathic. If there is clear evidence that what you are doing is not being enjoyed, stop at once and try something else. Don't get annoyed. Find out what is going on at school, so that he knows you are interested in his life even when he isn't with you—but be careful not to step on his own mother's preserves.

I was lucky. I don't think Andrew liked me much, and he was really beset by the matter of loyalty to his mother. We were very different, she and I. But there were things I could do that the boy respected. I could help him with French and with Latin, although I could not, like his mother, sing very well; I could not sew, dress fashionably, or make up my face properly. I was not immediately warm, nor did I have a low, husky, even sexy voice. But I could cook, and loved to, and I could hold my own with Andrew's father when we played word games. I could even match him quote for quote from Shakespeare or the Romantic poets. And I could play chess. Recently Andrew told his father that as a child one thing he'd respected about me was the chess. Of course as the years of prep school, college, and graduate school spun by, it all changed, and my meager intellectual attainments were far surpassed. But by then the roles were set, our experiences together rehashed and self-analyzed many times over, our judgments formed.

Andrew between 9 and 13 cared only superficially for my approval—and then only because life was easier if he had it. My own two boys minded if I scolded them or was clearly annoyed or made unhappy. Not he, though he was greatly annoyed, as was his father, by what he called "my look"— I suppose a frozen face of disapproval is trying beyond bearing. It took me many years to adjust to this indifference as to what I thought right and wrong. Naively, I thought justice and the good ought to triumph—but apparently this wasn't so. Besides, it was only *my* idea of justice. They have a different one!

It wasn't long before Noah and I fell into the habit of leaving Nick in charge when we went out (of course Mrs. White or someone was always around, but I mean in terms of between the boys themselves and their doings). This was a major mistake. If Andrew wasn't able to be sufficiently responsible, then we should have made sure the adult in the house was overseeing them more closely. To return home after being out and ask Nick, as Noah did, whether everything was all right and whether Andrew had behaved himself—the very idea today makes me shudder!

Yes, Andrew was naughty, was scolded, was more often than not in process of being punished. But he was loved. In our family, the situation of Cinderella in the fairy tale was not the case. Sometimes, true, it is, and then the stepmother and her children take over control of the household and the relationships involved, and as a united front call the tune on weekends as well as at other times. Then it is the stepchild, the visitor, who is made to feel unhappy, intrusive, unwanted, and the creator of problems for his father, who may only wish for a quiet life without conflict. This kind of stepmother, if there are any who have read thus far, should stop and consider what she is doing to a child deprived of his father for most of his waking hours. And she should work harder at including the child within the circle of her own children. I say "should," and have no business doing so, seeing all the mistakes I made in my particular situation. I mean merely to suggest a method of acting.

There are obvious problems and points of stress in the early days of forging a new family unit. Perhaps it might be useful to list here the everyday

sort of things that can cause trouble (although I
will be going into them in more detail as they
came up in my own story):
- meals and eating habits
- attitudes towards adults
- attitudes towards norms of behavior
- how he gets on with other children
- how he gets on with siblings in the family circle
- general behavior to those in authority
- how he behaves to his stepmother, both alone
    and in front of grown-ups or other children
- bedtime
- how you kiss him goodnight
- what he is going to call you
- "my mother lets me . . ."

VI

And so there was a pattern set, during those early years. Weekdays, Mondays through Thursdays, were quiet, uneventful, and unexciting—blessedly unexciting. Nick and Sam breakfasted and left for neighborhood schools by 8:30, and Noah for his office around 9:30. The days were mine, with free lance writing or research jobs to occupy me, the marketing, jovial exchanges with shopkeepers, cooking, housework, and the fun of exploring the old picturesque Heights area. I liked the solitude and mostly kept to myself in the day. But I was home when school let out—after that period between husbands of a nine-to-five desk job, I was happy to welcome the boys on their return, share their romps before supper, look over their homework, and listen to the day's adventures and tales of prowess or mishap. In fact, there was a pretty normal life during the week, and by and large the wheels of the household rolled smoothly along.

It all went into a different gear at mid-day Friday, when Andrew came, and, to continue the metaphor, traveled on high octane gas into the bargain. Sometimes—all too frequently as time went on—Andrew was kept in at school. In those days (I don't know what the practice is today) Collegiate School disciplined the boys due for punishment by making them sit silent in a classroom, inactive and unoccupied, Friday afternoon when everyone else went off to home or to the athletic field. For one as kinetic as Andrew, it was probably as difficult a punishment as they could devise. But Noah thought it too lenient and ineffective, and superimposed his own. More of that later.

Friday supper the boys ate upstairs. More fun for them, more noise permitted, more punctual (no knowing exactly what time Noah would be home), and simpler food, we told ourselves. It was also, of course, so that we could have our own cocktail and dinner in peace and quiet.

The summer Noah and I were married, I retained, along with his house, Elizabeth, the previous cleaning lady, to whom its dust-hiding nooks and crannies were familiar. But it was a mistake, and I had the sense finally to put an end to it. The temptation to talk of, or listen to, how things were in the previous tenant's reign, how badly Andrew behaved when . . . , and so on, were overpowering, but left an undignified and unpleasant cloud in the mind and distasteful questions asked, or at least thought of, on the lip (what a pyrrhic bolstering of one's own opinions). I changed the situation, and Mrs. White, Elizabeth's sister-in-law, came to us and "lived in," on the top floor with the boys. White-haired and dignified, she was so soft spoken the boys couldn't even hear her unless they were still. Harsh disciplinary methods or cross words were quite foreign to her. She had a sense of humor, a lovely feeling for the ridiculous, and a way of expressing herself that appealed to small boys. When her brother, also white-haired, came to visit her, she introduced him to them as General Nuisance, and as such, a perfectly sensible name to them, was he known.

Mrs. White governed, not by ukase but by affection, and by the very sweetness and innocence of her own personality. When she said her head ached, the boys were really sorry, and all of them, Andrew included, tried to be quieter. To her fell the task of seeing to it that Andrew wasn't too disruptive, that he didn't, for example, seize for himself the others' share of his favorite food—to which they, to keep the peace and because they seemed to accept his ascendancy over them, were perfectly prepared to yield.

I did, I think now, grow to look for trouble. Who's to say what really came first, *my* seeking out problems posed by a boy who was strange to me and hostile in his attitude, or *his* need to impress on me and on his father and stepbrothers that he was different, was a person who was important, to be listened to, even if only for two days out of the seven? Andrew didn't seem to mind whether it was approval he won, or a scolding, just so long as attention was riveted on him. But who will blame a child who has suddenly been dispossessed of his own house, his old neighborhood, his father, and all that was familiar, for *five* days out of the seven?

Alas, my reaction was often one of frustration and disapproval. I hadn't a clue that *expressed* feelings, whether cheerful or unhappy, were better than those *suppressed*. (How Nick would have benefited, had this not been so.) And I never quite understood that a troubled child, somehow knowing you are ready for the clash with him— no matter how desperately underneath it all he may yearn for your approval in order to gain his father's—will go about obliging you and create that confrontation.

The raucous shouts of laughter and loud talk from the third floor often took on a rather hysterical note. On Andrew's part because he was giving a performance, to be heard downstairs if possible as well as up, by Nick and Sam because they were fascinated by the bravado and excitement generated by their older brother, impressing him, they hoped, by *their* noise and naughtiness, and perhaps hoping to cash in on some of the consequent attention, yet with a percentage of apprehension as to the form it might take. And of course they all enjoyed pulling my leg, easy prey that I was (Noah didn't fall so easily, naturally). More than once I'd hear anguished sounds from above and bound upstairs, sure that Sammy was being mistreated (this did happen on occasion), to find him pretending to have been beaten up, but instead lying on the floor helpless with laughter.

When all the boys were in Brooklyn, the weekend program was erratic. But every other weekend, when Nick and Sam went to Long Island, I found it painful to realize that the air was balmier, sometimes even sunny (it seemed that the week was pleasant and easy without Andrew; the weekend, smoother and stress less likely without Nick and Sam). I was on occasion excluded, yes; but because Andrew was not fighting for his father's ear and eye and felt secure in holding both, the atmosphere was more loving and he was less likely to merit his father's wrath or my disapproval. When with adults, a single child is likely to act like an adult. Children together have a far better time of it playing up to each other, when there are more than one of them. When I was included, on these weekends with just three of us, it was because both Noah and Andrew wanted me.

Saturday mornings Noah slept late. Over his special once-a-week baked eggs and ham (his favorite Saturday breakfast to this day) he began his inviolate devouring of *The New York Times*. Any hopes the boys had of sharing morning hours with him were futile. While he read all the fine print, they danced on one foot or the other. But he paid no attention to their antics and suddenly it was lunch time. In the afternoon we did do things with them—sometimes. When it was fine, a game of catch perhaps, a walk on the waterfront, a Dodger ball game, followed almost always by that picnic over the living-room fire. It is amusing that today only Noah, with his romantically colored spectacles, thinks back fondly to the memory—of the coffee table pulled up near the hearth, the cannel coal crackling blue before sinking into the red ashes satisfactory for grilling, and those three short-cropped and shiny-faced small boys in bathrobe and pajamas, brandishing skewers and waiting their turn to roast.

Whether it was true or not, today Andrew believes his one aim was destruction—and he usually succeeded, whether it was of the mood of hope against hope that it all might turn out to be fun after all; or an actual plate that fell and broke on the slate hearth, its hot dog and roll and baked beans mingling on the carpet's edge; a stool overturned, a glass of milk spilt, the whole liberally watered at last by first blood—my tears—and accompanied by the full orchestra of his father's wrath.

Yet this destructiveness of Andrew's was aimed at adults, or rather, at a *situation*, which he found impossible to handle. He *never* tried to make mischief between the boys, or between them and their mother or stepfather. All three boys, whatever their feelings of sibling rivalry, jealousies, resentments, were loyal to each other—really each other's best booster. Andrew too did not complain to his father about his mother, or vice versa (if he had a problem with either, yes, he might *consult* the other). He was not a troublemaker of this kind. Trite as it sounds, I do believe there is truth to the idea that boys are more direct in their relationships than girls, less devious, not *bitchy*.

Weekends, there were shouting, sulks, and tears. But there were good times too (and I don't think it's just *my* rosy tinted glasses), when Noah played a recording by Basil Rathbone of "The Cask of Amontillado," or read poetry or something from "The Crock of Gold." There was a one-room delicatessen on Montague Street, called Sunny's, that was cheerful and informal enough to survive invasion from a family such as ours, where sometimes in spring or Indian summer we would eat on Saturday night instead. Noah gave the boys their first lesson in how to flirt, as he joked with the pert and pretty waitresses.

"Hello, Baby," he greeted one or the other; "What's good today that you're hiding?" and we would look over the menu and chafe as the boys took forever over their decisions. Not that their choices ever changed.

"I suppose you want your usual hamburger?" Noah would charge Nick, who couldn't deny it; and I can hear today Andrew's request:

"Chicken soup with lots of matzoh balls," he'd order. When the girl returned, she'd say, "Here's your matzoh balls with soup." And sure enough, she had brought him three or four dumplings instead of the usual two, crowding out of sight the amber liquid of the broth.

    Sam's tastes were less conservative than his older brother's. "Cream soda and corned beef sandwich for me and my father here," Noah would say with complete seriousness as the boys dissolved into giggles. "And a new pickle." Always the new pickle. Sometimes we sent the boys to Sunny's on their own (the proprietor's name was really Joe, now retired in Florida) and some time later, for they all had to exchange the time of day with him and their friends the waitresses, they would return with packages of corned beef, pastrami, bread slices, new pickles, and containers of the special mustard hoarded by delicatessens and impossible to find elsewhere. We would spread it all out and apportion it, then sit companionably on our front stoop watching the world go by as we ate. Saturday night, too, usually meant chocolate fudge cake from Ebinger's, eaten with milk when the boys quieted down before bedtime. To this day my family remembers that cake with nostalgia and slavering jaws, but I haven't found a chocolate fudge anywhere in the city so satisfactory to them, and long ago I gave up trying to concoct one of my own, after many disastrous efforts.

Sunday, after our special pancakes or French toast brunch, came the matter of kitchen duty. When Nick and Sam were on Long Island for the weekend and Andrew was alone with us, there was little problem in cleaning up. I took care of it willingly. But when the five of us had eaten, the mess that remained was a different matter. Noah was not at all like poor cousin Maud's husband Norman when it came to chores in the house. As a matter of course the two older boys dealt with the remains of breakfast, one washing and the other drying in turns. But it was rarely smooth going, and Andrew's sulks and studied carelessness in contrast to Nick's way of getting it all done easily and without fuss made Noah fume. The size of the mini-kitchen didn't make the boys' task any easier. I'll never forget when poor Andrew upset the coffee can of waste fat onto the top of the stove and down its sides. The boy was filled with consternation, while Noah's wrath echoed through the living room. I quickly shoved the boys out to play in the shelter of the dingy yard and cleaned it up myself.

The boys enjoyed the neighborhood in which we lived. Andrew in those early years still had friends from the time he had lived there. Sometimes, in a show of older brother independence, off he'd go with them. Nick was beginning to make friends at his school and Sam, the little fair-skinned blue-eyed charmer, would cheerfully ride by himself round and round the block on Andrew's old tricycle, now refurbished in light blue paint. When he was a little older, he roamed the St. George Hotel with his friend Billy, son of the manager. What he liked most in those years was, in the way of small boys, the errands he could do for Mrs. White and myself. Best of all was a trip to Mr. Semple's fancy grocery.

"What's on your mind, if any?" he'd be greeted by the proprietor. Once he'd worked this one out, the sally would break him up for an hour. The greeting was invariable, and so was his enjoyment of it.

When children are brought together through their parents' remarriage, the one who is an only child will probably have the devil's own time of it, so much is he suddenly deprived of what he had to himself before. I think what made our family life so particularly difficult, what made it almost impossible for me to cope successfully with the problem of Andrew, was the fact that for eight years he had had the rewards and attentions as well as the disadvantages of an only child. He couldn't share, for he had never had to. It was really not until he went to boarding school that he learned this lesson (made easier there because those he was forced to share with and take into consideration were not members of his family). Even in camp during the summer months he tried to be ahead of others, or apart—not quite one of them.

This was dramatized for us sharply when, our second summer, we took a shot at a family holiday—no camp, no children sent away from us. Rather, we all went off to my mother's summer family house, then empty, on a remote island off the Maine coast, with rough seas, rocks, woods, and sharply piney air. I have always loved this place, and I looked forward to my new husband and son's doing so too. Why could not its alchemy achieve a miracle, the welding of a family?

But while there were many good moments and many pastimes that we all enjoyed together, it didn't really work. Andrew was too individualistic still, too keen to hog the limelight—the rest of us too anxious, for example, when he took the axe to cut down a tree and everything and everyone around was in danger because he would not be disciplined and controlled about it. He copped out of chores whenever possible, making them seem a drag beneath contempt, instead of a participation in grown-up doings, which the younger boys even enjoyed. When we had for supper the fresh lobsters still wet from the salty ocean, he always demanded more than his share—and sulked when denied. Perhaps it didn't work for him because he was too much a city boy, like his father before him. Only now, in my husband's middle age, do the fish in our pond, the deer at twilight seen from our window, the ants busy around the anthill, our moonlit fields and woods, an oriole's call, or the infinite variety of leaf and tree, mean something to him. If perhaps he and I together had been able to convey to Andrew that summer our present wonder and delight in nature, maybe he'd have slowed up and begun to look at things outside himself.

Laughter is a wondrous harmonizer, welder, healer, breaker of tensions, and remover of conflicts. My happiest memory of that miserable Maine summer in the midst of much loved surroundings, was the affair of the chocolate pudding. Instant foods were just then coming on the market, and instead of buying the old My-T-Fine or Royal, one day my hand picked up a new product. It was called Amazo, a chocolate powder to which one merely added milk and stirred, and lo and behold a delicious pudding. No more stirring over the stove in the struggle to avoid lumps, no more waiting for it to cool and solidify, no more pudding too solid or too runny.

We ate it for supper and the verdict was "delicious." "Absolutely Amazo," said Andrew, and we all laughed.

Next day at the small fresh water lake, Nick executed a perfect jackknife. "Amazo," Andrew told him when his head reappeared above the surface. I thought the boy would drown, he laughed so hard, and Sam almost fell off the dock. We all broke up, Noah and I included. For the rest of the summer the same rollicking hilarity could be evoked at will, and was. "Amazo!" was the comment most often heard. That it had been Andrew who thought of the joke made us all laugh the harder, and the adults appreciate it particularly. The change from scoldings or disapproval was tacitly refreshing to us all.

Nevertheless, we decided that the Maine experiment had not been a success, and for six more summers the boys went to camp.

The matter of dealing with two families at once is understandably disturbing for a child, and the adults around him often don't realize just how much. Andrew came to us by subway Friday afternoon from school, whence he had gone by school bus from his mother's apartment that morning. He took the return journey to school by subway Monday morning—back to another borough and another life. And it was on Mondays that he ran against the school's grain, and tumbled into his worst trouble spot. Somehow the underlying knowledge of this change in environment was more than physical, and it shook him up in chaotic fashion. It was the unusually wise and helpful Wilson Parkhill, Headmaster of Collegiate, who came to this conclusion and pointed it out to us, and it proved a useful clue even though it came a bit late in the game (Mr. Parkhill had doubtless plenty of experience with children from "broken homes," so that the pattern of disturbance must have been an old story to him).

Nick and Sam must have undergone similarly troubling symptoms, but they controlled them more easily. Perhaps it helped that they only experienced this upheaval every two weeks. In any case there were no overt conflicts between their two households.

The traumatic aspects behind forcing a child to adjust to a different home life once a week is accentuated, of course, by the attitude of those at each end of the subway line. It is they who have the power to put the new arrival in tune or out of tune with the changed surroundings. I tried hard not to question or criticize any element of Andrew's other life, and the same for Nick and Sam. I am sure the boys' other parents did likewise (it's a neat trick to do this, and still make a boy feel you are interested in all aspects of his life and would like to share it if he wishes). But children are acute. Of course there was criticism implied, plenty of times—in my not allowing Andrew to eat three lamb chops or ten chicken wings, and nothing else, "as my mother does," for example. I know how put out I was when Sam came home from Long Island one time, to chatter happily for days about the "delicious pineapple upside down cake" Ann had made (it is not something I would ever conceive of attempting, but I was jealous, I suppose, of his admiration for his stepmother's concoction). It didn't occur to me that the humorous and grandiose title was itself a cause for amusement to a 6-year-old, and that he might even not have cared particularly for the dessert itself. Not that that matters. Jealousy to a greater or lesser degree is almost inevitable among and between all these parents. Queensberry rules between them are hard to keep when each has her or his own firm ideas about child rearing, care of property, manners, consideration of others, sportsmanship—all of these were of importance to me, and I wanted to instill them in my boys. I'm sure the other parents had precepts they believed in that were equally valid, perhaps even more so than mine.

But I was concerned with bringing my children up in a certain way, and Andrew's contemptuous approach to my ideas, whether real or not (and out of some sort of loyalty if not self-defense, held by his father too) both troubled me and was resented by me. When Nick once returned from a park outing with Andrew and his mother, to report to me, because it bothered him, that Andrew had thrown his new gloves into the reservoir and they had all forthwith gone shopping for another pair, I held my peace, much as I wanted to express myself. I felt virtuous. It didn't occur to me that perhaps this was a way of dealing with Andrew's problem that wasn't necessarily wrong—in fact might have been the best way to handle it. But it did pose a question to me, that must arise often with this sort of family equation: how to be wise, tolerant, and outwardly uncritical and fair to absent "other parents," yet instill one's own but contradictory precepts in the children? Not easy.

Because Andrew posed more problems than a bucketful of jumping frogs, he inevitably had more attention paid to him by myself, Noah, and most other adults also. Conversely, Nick, who was two years his junior, but who had to compete on Andrew's level in order to be accepted by him and Noah, had far less attention and was the chorus of one in the background. He was the "good" child. We were never at our wit's end about him, never spent hours talking with him and about him, going over his problems, deciding what should be done, never had important sessions of solemn talk with him, his teachers, his headmaster. I am on the point of writing "never had knockdown fights over him," but that is not true—in fact Noah and I may have had more disagreements over him than about Andrew, since Andrew's happiness and serenity was something we both desired and were united in working towards (for our own sakes, of course, too, because when things went wrong with him we all suffered). We were not worried about Nick; he presented no problem to us; he was rarely the center of our attention, at least during this period. He seemed to have no problems, at least no outward manifestation of them (of course he *had* them), and so he could be dismissed from our minds, in the sense of troubling us. This naturally made me unhappy, as did each occasion that Noah was less interested in something to do with him than in Andrew. How foolish of me to mind. He got straight A's in school, was well liked, a leader in his class, a star performer in athletics and school plays. Noah used to comment sometimes about Nick's competitiveness. How could it be otherwise, I thought resentfully, when his presence and participation was suffered only if it was on Andrew's level—an Andrew two years his senior and bright and intelligent at that? Small wonder that he was competitive, and pretty successfully, too. It was the old Tom Sawyer, Huck Finn approach. The good boy just doesn't seem as interesting as those who get into trouble all the time, in the picturesque fashion of Huck or Tom. Not that Nick was a self-satisfied do-gooder like Cousin Sid.

This brings me to a warning—one that I'd give anything for someone to have passed on to me at the right time. Don't neglect your own children— don't neglect *any* child, if it comes to that—just because they are familiar with and accept your pattern for them, your precepts, your standards, your demands for them, and so don't trouble you or make trouble for you. I think I regret today as much my failures over Nick as those over Andrew. Andrew wished for our consuming interest, and succeeded in holding it riveted to his crew-cut head. It was more challenging to read on a report: "Andrew has a fine mind—potentially. His attention wanders, however, and he could apply himself more. He is careless and sloppy. A good student—when he tries." One could do something with this.

But where can you go, or what can you do, with

straight A's? You become almost bored, it is so automatic, and you dismiss it with, "That's just fine, Nicky." Of course, I wasn't bored, I just pretended to be; and I didn't feel for a minute like dismissing it. But I was self-conscious about it, in the face of Andrew's situation, and did not wish to delight in my son's success in case Noah would feel even more unhappy about Andrew. But I wonder that Nick didn't stop working altogether, so that we'd ask him what had happened, and even scold him a little. The boy may even have wished that he'd do badly once in a while, to get our attention. That there were danger areas around both boys was not as obvious as it should have been. It was only too easy to neglect or shortchange such a responsive and responsible little boy. I was guilty of doing just that.

One such occasion comes to mind. Nick must have been 9 or 10 when he had to have his tonsils out. At this time he was sweet-natured, dark and thin, eager to please and eager to learn, responsible enough to take himself and little brother on the Long Island Railroad alone, but a charmer as well, with prune eyes, thatch of dark hair, and the olive skin of Italian cherubs. The operation necessitated a night in the hospital. I stayed with him until late, but he was still asleep from the anesthetic. The doctor assured me he would remain so until morning. Noah expected me home and had let me know it in no uncertain terms. I left, to hold together that fortress that I somehow stupidly believed would fall apart without me. How silly and senseless. I should have realized that a stepparent will automatically worry less about his stepson and feel it less important for his wife to be with him in the hospital. I should have realized this, and listened instead to my own gut reaction, knowing that my place was with the child.

Many years later Nick told me, in an uncharacteristically articulated display of resentment against me, that he'd woken up, dry-throated, sore, frightened, and alone in the night. He needed me. He could get no nurse to come, no one to hear his hoarse call. He lay there trying not to cry painfully to himself. He did not say a word about it when he returned home. But he'd held it against me, understandably, for many years.

When Andrew had had his tonsils out some years before, there had been no question that his mother stay at his side throughout the night. His father thought this right and natural, and because it was *his* son, he felt the knife rasping against his own throat and wished he could take the boy's place. The difference between Andrew's mother and myself was not that she had more love for her son than I for mine, but that at moments when her showing that love were necessary, when he needed her open proof of it, it was there. She was not caught up in a continuing balancing act of devotion to child and husband that the woman in a second marriage is more likely to be attempting. Again my own traitorous upbringing that led me to over-emphasize self-reliance. That essentially one is alone, yes; and early knowledge of this girds one for life. But surely not more so than the certainty of parental love in a time of crisis?

VII

 That Andrew was a troubled child was clear to Noah and me—in fact to all the adults who came in contact with him. It was not only for her own peace of mind, and her career, but also—or perhaps chiefly—because she hoped it would make for a more settled life for him, that his mother moved to California. It was certainly not because she wanted to give up her son! I have already described the boy's extreme loyalty to both parents, to the point perhaps of its being the main reason why he could not behave well for any length of time *with* either of them and thus was not an unalloyed joy *to* either of them. Noah and I understood this. We believed Andrew would not be able to settle down with us, be at peace with us, while his mother was in California. He would be even less able to deal with himself—consumed with surface guilts over day-to-day behavior that he might think was the reason why she didn't take him with her—and might even feel that he

had in effect been responsible for chasing her away. We looked for some other solution.

Where could we find for him an objective environment, in which his very real gifts and powers would find direction and scope, unhindered by family roadblocks, where the muscles of mind and body could develop to the fullest (a favorite concept of Noah's)? We began to look into the matter of prep schools.

We also knew that our lives would be smoother, easier, less concentrated on Andrew and his troubles if he were not with us all in the Brooklyn house. A boarding school product myself, I held firmly that an adolescent male matures best in a monastic society (today I am not so convinced as I was), with peers, masters, bull sessions, a full athletic program, all of it away from the tugging and fretting of the city world with its tinsel pleasures and titillations from which even a schoolboy is not immune. Being nothing if not intellectual snobs, Noah and I wanted the best for Andrew, and we thought that Exeter was the best.

But Collegiate would not recommend Andrew for Exeter or Exeter for Andrew—although he was by this time academically one of their most promising pupils. He was not "mature" enough, they said, for that New Hampshire institution where boys were left pretty much on their own as regards curriculum and pastimes. They felt that under all the circumstances surrounding his family life, a school providing more of a guiding hand would be preferable. They recommended Hotchkiss. Late in the summer Noah and I took Andrew up for an interview and to see whether we liked the place.

I was beginning to consolidate my thoughts about what has become rather a pet theory of mine—that children in "broken home" situations should often have their own blood parent to themselves, without benefit of stepfather or stepmother or stepbrothers. Noah didn't take this very seriously, although I tried on this occasion to persuade him it would be best for him to make the journey with Andrew on his own. This visit to a boy's school, a man's world and so on, surely I could wait to see it all later? Besides, if I wasn't around, Andrew's impressions and attitudes towards the place would be less structured; if I expressed approval or appreciation over some aspect, he might not want to oppose me even though he didn't like it. Still, I was overruled. The school itself, I believe, agreed with me, since one of the big events of the year was Father's Weekend—no mothers allowed.

We were impressed. Noah formed an instant

kinship and identification with the school which prevented him from ever seeing it again without benefit of rose-colored glasses. We were drawn to the kindly craggy-faced headmaster, the Rev. Thomas Chappell, we admired the red-bricked dormitory buildings and sunny classrooms, attractive dining room, and student-filled, well-stocked, functional library. In spite of, or perhaps even because of, the unequivocal austerity of the place—the boys' rooms were virtual cells—our reaction, even Andrew's, was positive, and we decided to enter him in the ninth grade for the following year, when he would be 14. As added bonus we discovered that the teacher of Latin and Greek had once been a pupil of my father's. This created a tangible bond, to begin with, later reinforced by Andrew and Nick's study of the Classics throughout their four years under this man. His unassailable scholarship, dry wit, and unassuming air make him perhaps the most respected master at the school.

To be accepted Andrew had to achieve a certain success in his work at Collegiate, for even at that time competition for places was becoming very keen (nothing approaching that of today, however). Later in the autumn the application forms came for us to fill in—again this was before the day of nerve-wracking SAT examinations for children of seventh and eighth grades today who hope to enter private secondary schools. I was amazed to find on those forms, under the heading of *Parents,* spaces for *separated, divorced;* and in addition to spaces for the names of father and mother, room also for *stepfather* and *stepmother.*

That year, when Andrew was in the eighth grade and his mother was on the other side of the continent, I tried to enter more into his school life. But I found it embarrassing, our relationship awkward. At times when parents appeared to be with their sons, I went: at plays, teas, Prize Day, Parents' Day; Noah made every effort to attend the more academic functions, such as Class Day, when parents sat in on actual classroom work. Since my last name was the same as Andrew's, our complicated relationship was not immediately obvious to the uninitiated; his friends could greet me simply with, "Hello, Mrs. Joplin," and no mutual embarrassment. Later, when Sam attended Collegiate, it was different. "Hello, Mrs. Links," a 10-year-old would say brightly, only to be corrected by my son: "Her name is Mrs. Joplin." The boy, realizing his mistake, would retreat in confusion, Sam and I grin at each other in embarrassment, or pointedly look away from each other.

I don't suppose Andrew particularly liked my visiting Collegiate, though he never expressed this. But I can remember attending a basketball game against another school, during which my stepson would not once look in my direction, although I had made my presence known at the beginning. I naturally wondered if it was worth it, my trying in this way to show I was interested and cared, and if I were doing the right thing. When I showed him that I knew how the school stood competitively in various sports, when I knew his friends' names and what happened to them, and remembered where they lived and what he had said about them, he was pleased, I think, in spite of himself, especially since Noah never remembered any of this sort of detail. The extra effort was well worth while.

Friday evening was homework time—theoretically most of it was supposed to be completed before Noah asked about it, and I well recall quizzing Andrew on his French and Latin, becoming impatient over his lack of memory, his careless mistakes and devil-may-care attitude. But I also remember, with the whole family lying around him on the living-room floor, our helping him on Aristophanes' *Frogs*, the project he had selected that month in Ancient History. Noah was the expert here, but we all made suggestions for the giant chart-map-drawing Andrew made with its differently colored legends and symbols. It was a marvelous moment of union, enjoyed by all of us. Loud were the boys' howls when Noah read the play aloud at some of the more raucous scatological parts.

Except where it touched Andrew, Nick didn't often have the benefit of this kind of family involvement. There was little need, and no impulse to initiate it. One doesn't place oneself in a situation where rejection is likely very often.

When Andrew was about 14, and Nick 12, the older boy chided me. "You never praise Nicky," he said. It was true. While there was nothing to chide him about, and much to praise, there was with the younger boy so little to balance the constant criticism dished out to Andrew or warranted but bitten back, that whenever possible I would jump on Nick, and since praise would have to be constant, I doubtless refrained completely. And with Andrew, because there was so much to blame him for, to correct, to caution, when a moment for praise came, he got it with double the enthusiasm.

When I visited Nick's school, I would be embarrassed by the chorus of adulation from teachers and other parents alike. Underneath it all, I was, of course, fantastically proud of my son; I would beam back, and mutter something deprecating as I backed away. But my guilt towards Andrew and Noah for my resentment at the constant need to "work" with the boy, put out excessive effort in understanding, in patience, in attention, all this forced me to downgrade Nick and resulted in my shortchanging him altogether.

During this period Andrew had friends at Collegiate, and still some in the neighborhood of the house in Brooklyn. It is strange that today he remembers it as a time without friends; but I don't forget easily the boy at school who had a way of sparking Andrew's mischievous proclivities, so that when he wasn't starting something, Seth was. There was Tony, and Billy too. All of them came to the house. It was, rather, I believe now, the newness of brotherhood and the intense quality of the relationships in our house, the self-consciousness of all of us towards our roles to each other as time went on, that precluded an easy coming and going of outsiders. During the first years when Andrew was with us only on weekends, and during that final year when he lived in Brooklyn with all of us, the boys from school did come down with him. But a subway ride is no pleasure, and once they had seen the house and what it offered, their curiosity if not their energy evaporated. Andrew did also go to their homes sometimes after school—when he was not being kept in—but as much to avoid the lunchtime with me as for any other reason.

Yet the impression left with Andrew is that he had no friends. Actually, I think he was far more interested in those inside our house than out; introducing other elements into it only complicated matters. Nick too didn't begin to bring friends to the house until Andrew was away at boarding school.

I also believe that in spite of the prevalence of divorce in the United States, and in New York City and its environs in particular, many people do disapprove of the institution—even if they don't realize this themselves—to the point of making their attitude quite plain. Perhaps to these people, Andrew was less welcome now that his parents were divorced.

When I went to Collegiate, I was Andrew's stepmother to those in the know; this meant his teachers certainly, and some other parents, besides Andrew's coterie of friends. I was his stepmother, and it showed, like the slightly soiled white edge of a slip hanging beneath a skirt. Something a little sordid, maybe even shameful and illegitimate. I was aware of it almost all of the time, and so was Andrew. It was an awareness constantly with us whenever we were in a public

situation. I retain a sharply unhappy memory—
not of a particular incident, merely a feeling—
of trying to strike up an acquaintance with the
parents of Andrew's best friend that year, without
success. This had happened in Brooklyn, too,
with neighbors who had been friendly with his
parents before their divorce. But I had put this
down to the fact that the boys no longer went to
school together or enjoyed the same experiences.
I even thought the parents might just plain not
like me. But the Collegiate parents had no chance
to like or dislike, since they had never met me.
This was only the first of such experiences.

When Andrew's mother dismantled her New
York apartment and moved to California she gave
the old Dumont TV set to her son. Together
with his battered teddy bear, his baseball mitt,
chinos, and blue buttondowns, he brought it to
Brooklyn. Down it went to the basement playroom. I bought three black iron-framed sling
chairs, with canvas seats of green, orange, and
black, so that the boys could sit in comfort in
front of the monster. When homework (and
poetry learning) were done, the boys were allowed
to watch for a while. We didn't like the whole
idea much, but short of rationing hours, we didn't
wish to take away from Andrew something he
had enjoyed at his mother's. Anyway, their

homework had become so heavy, there really wasn't too much time that the two older boys could spend watching television.

What Andrew did with the chairs, my reaction, his irritation with my reaction, his father's mild annoyance that it bothered me so that I picked on Andrew, his anger at Andrew for bugging me and not paying attention to my requests or else forgetting them, Noah's finally being furious with both me and his son, my resentment and self-pity and squirming at the injustice I felt—all of this gives a picture in microcosm of the kinds of petty matters that caused the mutual resentment and hostility between Andrew and myself to flare.

First of all the boy would plunk himself down in the sling, hard enough to break anything less sturdy. Immediately he'd tilt it forward so that his canvas-supported bottom rested on the floor, or almost on the floor. But he wouldn't stay there, instead swayed up and down, closer to the position the chair was supposed to be in, with its back legs firmly on the floor—or off, with the canvas seat touching the floor. Naturally, this had the effect of straining the canvas sling, whose corners, doubled over and stitched pocket-fashion, held it on the frame. It wasn't long before these corners frayed. It was some time longer before they tore, but their raggedy edges served to remind me of my resentment, even when Andrew was not in the room. I tried to stop him, of course. But he couldn't, or wouldn't. Then I tried to make him stick to one color, so that the other slings would stay "nice," and Nick and Sam have unfrayed chairs to sit in. I met with no success; Andrew just couldn't see what I was fussing about, cared less, and thus never remembered. When Noah began to be angry with me, as well as with Andrew, I stopped. But the whole bit rankled, and does to this day when I see Andrew tilt a chair, or catch sight of a raggedy sling out on our lawn.

By this time Cindy was part of the family—a black woolly bundle of sentimentality that I had found for the boys at the Ellen Prince Speyer Home for Animals (in the days before it was part of Cornell Medical). I had gone there, after long discussions with Noah in which we had concluded that a dog mght cement relationships—and anyway boys needed a dog, didn't they? My object was to find a male, smooth-haired puppy to give the three of them at Christmas. It was then Christmas week. I returned to Noah, reporting that we had bought a dog in every respect the opposite of what I had set out for, but the best $3.00 I had ever spent. (It turned out that, inadvertently, I had bought a purebred

Hungarian puli.) Noah and I fetched her Christmas Eve, all necessary shots having been taken care of, and hid her in the basement, steeling our hearts against her whimpering through the night alone.

Early next morning, while the boys were busy emptying stockings filled with tangerine, silver dollar, nuts, a tiny box of raisins, and many small treasures, we tied a string to the Christmas tree in the living room, trailed it through the hall and round the corner to the basement stairs, down them to the playroom and fastened it onto the black Hungarian puli's collar—so that when the moment came, the boys could play treasure hunt and find her.

Even strangers loved Cindy, and as for the family, she held a place secure in our hearts for the fifteen years she was with us. We called her Cinderella because she was black as coal; a little foundling among the ashes. Farfetched? But anyway, a stepsister, to go with three stepbrothers. Perhaps it was the way her black hair fell over her face, almost hiding her soft appealing liquid eyes that made her irresistible, or the wiggle of ecstasy she gave, even when no longer a puppy, when almost anyone showed an interest in her, or the puddle she'd make if certain people, particularly males, were kind enough to talk to her or pat her. She was the kind of dog who was so intrinsically good she made everyone within her orbit good too, like a dear Chinese friend of ours. She looked like a woolly mop, though her hair was fine and silky and the devil to comb.

The boys, Andrew in particular, loved her on sight. Unlike the others, he had already had a dog, who had run away. And he had an immediate and moving and living object to hug, play with, fidget with, and romp with.

But while the success of our gift was clear from the moment the squealing trio of small boys followed the string to its end in the basement, Cindy did little to lessen our problems. Andrew, as the eldest, was the logical one to care for her. But the first year she was with us, he came only on weekends. And besides his memory was not to be counted on, he was too erratic. Sam was too little, and still not strong enough to take on such a responsibility. Nick, if I'd made him responsible, might have stirred up a rivalry with Andrew that, blessedly, didn't seem to exist, or at least was not on any sort of serious or vicious level.

Andrew loved the dog, in fact they appropriated each other, but even this was not enough to overcome his antagonism to discipline and training and routine that looking after a puppy necessitated.

And since Noah wasn't about to undertake all the chores required, the task fell to me. Of course. But apart from the nuisance of it all, the partnership was good for me—we were two females in a world of males. I valued her support, believe me.

What happens to a woman who is confronted with tense situations on a day-in, day-out basis? She exists, if she is like me, in a constant uptight state, relaxed only when her problems are in bed and asleep. Since part of each evening can be given over to rehashing what happens during the day, this can lead to the sort of bickering and outright battle Andrew would have enjoyed witnessing (to hear him tell it, anyway). Noah and I swung like monkeys hour by hour between tremendous empathy and satisfaction in our love and companionship, to quarrels I thought I couldn't bear a day longer. These arguments which the older boys could not have helped being aware of, and Andrew was frequently an instigator of, had the components many times capable of breaking up a marriage. I was more than once on the brink of leaving, and only the thought of putting Nick and Sam through the whole mess again stopped me. This aspect, must, it seems to me, serve as adhesive to many second marriages. Of course, there *were* other aspects too: the horror of putting myself through it all again as well, the sense of failure once again. And then perhaps a moment's pause, when blessings, positive ones, are counted? With the wide open road of opportunity narrowing as one grows older, those blessings become more valuable, their totting up surely acting as a brake.

Nevertheless, there were many bad moments. I even went so far, in a second of terrible aberration, to say to Nick, "Don't worry, darling, Noah and I won't get a divorce." He looked utterly shocked, and was speechless for a moment. Then he said that it had never occurred to him. I saw then how I was making a confidant of my older son to his certain detriment, no matter how he really, deep down, might have felt about such a prospect as our divorce. I vowed never to do so again, and prayed that he'd bury the careless remark or forget it entirely.

It was during this period of my life that my incipient but mild rheumatic and arthritic pains grew more acute. I don't know if other mothers of difficult stepchildren react in this way, but I found myself always tired and edgy, sorry for myself and aching in bone. Tension and stress result in fatigue, no doubt about it. If I was tired in the evening, I couldn't cope with possible bickering, or with any sort of stress surrounding supper and the hour or so before the boys' bedtime, with Noah still unrelaxed from his day's work. If I was not even-tempered and able to remain that way in the face of mild provocation, things tended to fall apart. I was oversensitive, overreactive, and so whenever possible, during the day, I rested. When I had to go somewhere, I took taxis. At home, I lay on the gray couch in the living room, facing the fireplace and the open door. And it was there I could usually be found, any time boys or man were home. Just as when my husband was at home he could be found in his favorite chair flanking the fireplace. As time went on, of course, and the boys departed in turn for boarding school, the strains and stresses, problems and tensions, grew less sharp and bothersome, and my miseries, if not vanishing completely, could at least be kept under control.

While Noah always felt more comfortable if all of us were together, and told himself and the rest of us quite often that we *were* a family and all loved each other, I slowly began to believe that an occasional rest from this very equation would be beneficial and restful for each one of us, a removing of competition, of built-in pressures. I was trying hard, by this time, to think through some of the problems that Andrew had, that I had, and that were inherent in our not very sound relationship. I also thought that so much highly charged atmosphere so much of the time was not very good for Nick and Sam.

I remember the first time that I was able to persuade Noah that we should put this theory of mine into effect. The plan was that he take Andrew to his office for the afternoon, with a meal and a picture gallery afterwards, while I ferry to Staten Island for a picnic with Nick and Sam in a park not too far from St. George and the ferry slip. Nick was already flexing his legs (he was to be a track star, the 100-yard dash in 10.3) and we ran races before we ate. I'll never forget the joy on my son's face—he was 10 or 11 at the time—when he beat me on the final effort. It made the day a million times worth the 30-cent fare we paid for round trip for three—though of course I pretended to be mortified.
Even Noah conceded that the experiment was a success and that my theory might have merit.

With summer coming up, once more we were faced with the question of camp. Andrew was to be 13 in August, Nick 11, and Sam was 9. We agreed on a change from the much loved Journey's End, and made plans for Andrew to go to a boys' camp in the Middle West—half way to his mother in California, in Michigan's Upper Peninsula; Nick and Sam were to go to a camp run by the athletics master at Friends School. And at the end of the 8-week period once again we would try out this separateness experiment—Noah would go to meet Andrew in Chicago and spend ten days or so there, and I would pick up Nick and Sam and take them to farm country in Pennsylvania.

This sort of separation into the natural relationship must, it seems to me, help to remove the sense of enforced sharing that occurs in the step-relationship but is not present in the normal blood family. Of course it is wise to teach children to be realistic when their parents break up and remarry other people; they must accept the fact that their father and mother will not reunite, that their life with stepbrothers and stepparent is the reality. But there can be a marvelous sense of freedom, of slackening off of reins held by a stepfather or stepmother, of getting out of the habit of quick resentments that, whether superficial or basic, are ready to flare out at the flick of a switch. For Andrew to have his father completely to himself, for Noah not to have to think of me, of whether Andrew was doing something to make me unhappy or that I thought wrong, for me not to worry lest he was leading the younger boys astray or tiring Sam, to wonder if I was being too hard on Andrew or neglecting Nick—all this could be nothing but salutary, I believed.

And there were the relatives. There were plenty on both sides, eager to see the boys—but only their own relations, not strangers. It is really too much to ask a nonrelative child to take on the deferential, polite mien obligatory for aunts, cousins, and assorted relations, too boring the talk of "when you were a baby, you used to . . . ," or "your mother did this," or "Grandma did that. . . ." Andrew was to visit his family in Chicago, Nick and Sam theirs in Towanda, Pennsylvania.

Of course our trial run turned out very different from expectation. What one doesn't? I left before my husband, to meet the boys near their camp. Noah telephoned Michigan to make arrangements for picking up Andrew, only to learn that one camper had come down with polio. This was during the early Salk period. There *was* vaccine, to be sure, but it was so new that everyone was not yet automatically injected. Andrew had of course been exposed. So Noah had the business of arranging for a special doctor who did have the vaccine; he had to see to it that the boy did not get overtired, while hiding his watching and his fear, so that this awful apprehension wasn't passed on to Andrew.

But there were some plusses to this turn of events as well—an emergency shared with Dad and Dad only, the being grown up with Dad and no little brothers to be considered, the visits to relatives in Chicago happily shortened without anyone's taking offense, and the coming home to a house with just the two of them in it. And of course no sharing of Dad with stepmother!

On my side, there were aspects of fiasco too, though it all ended well enough. I had thought a farm vacation would be unusual and fun, besides healthy, for these city children unfamiliar with the milking of cows and birthing of lambs. Since Nick at this time wished ardently to be an ornithologist when he grew up, and was teased about this by Noah, I thought he might learn some more about his pet project undisturbed by difficult currents. The Commerce Department of the State of New York puts out a booklet called *Farm Vacations*. One was listed there, not in New York state, but near my mother's home town of Towanda, Pennsylvania, where there were relatives living.

My first misgivings sneaked into awareness when we were picked up at the station after descending from the soot-encased, creaky old Black Diamond (the train I had taken to college near Ithaca and now rightly defunct). When no one else remained on the platform, I understood that our hosts were those two aged ladies, and an equally aged man (their brother, it turned out, who didn't even live on *their* farm). We were driven to the farm by its owners. The driver of the car was the daughter of one of the ladies, and I was horrified to learn that she lived some distance away and that there was no transportation of any kind linking the farm to some sort of civilization—such as a telephone booth, for example. I watched the daughter drive away, marooning us in deserted countryside, and my heart sank.

When we entered the rundown farmhouse and put down our bags in the enormous bedroom, dusty, cluttered, and antimacassared, and oddly strange and sinister, disappointment was hardly the word. I tried to assure the boys that we'd feel better after eating, that supper would be a wonderful country meal that they would love. We sat down at a round table with the two old ladies, who succeeded in being fluttery and silent at the same time. We looked at huge hunks of white bread, at butter that was brilliant yellow and tasted strange, at pale, skimmed milk that, it suddenly occurred to me, might not be pasteurized. I tried to eat a mouthful of the ham on my plate. It was too salty. The boys could hardly swallow their milk. Back in our room, whence we escaped as quickly as we decently could, Sam wasted no time in bursting into tears; Nick was close to it. I could only cheer them up by promising that we'd leave as soon as we could find a way to do so, and I set them to thinking of the problem as a puzzle—how were we to get away? Making a game of it worked, and we went to sleep in a more cheerful frame of mind.

Next day the weather was fine, fortunately, and we took a picnic lunch on our walk to the nearest town, some two miles away or more, where a telephone might be found. On our return, I told our hostesses that my aunt in Towanda was very ill (she was, quite truthfully, in a nursing home there) and that none of my relatives could understand why we were so far away. It took another day to get hold of the daughter so that she could drive us away, but I think we managed to leave without hurting the ladies irreparably. Consultations with my cousins resulted in our being taken to a pleasant lakeside inn not far away from their cabin in the woods. There was swimming, we were introduced to the Italian game of *bocci*, and we had plenty of good, familiar food without strange thin farm milk and butter. Our final week was a joy.

Even though the actual working out of my theory did not turn out to be a shining success for any of us, I still maintain its validity, to the point of making myself unpopular with some of my friends. I recommended it to a couple on the west coast, where I had gone for a quick trip. The father, a widower, and his daughter Amy were old friends whom I had not seen for some time. He had recently remarried, a darkly handsome, very intelligent and pleasant woman whom I took to immediately.

At dinner, Amy was silent, unresponsive and almost sulky. I asked her why, during a moment snatched alone when we were drying dishes.

"I can never talk to Daddy any more," she answered. "*She* guards him like a hawk, as though I were trying to take him away, or something. She's always there. If I ask him a question about homework, *she* answers. If I ask what is happening at the office (her father is Senior Editor of a publishing company), *she* answers. He lets her run his life, for Pete's sake. He never goes out with his friends any more; he's always at home. With *her*. It's awful."

"Why don't you have lunch with him once a week," I suggested. "I'm sure he'd love it, and you could catch up with each other that way. Shall I suggest it?"

"Oh please, yes." Amy was delighted. I was making a mistake, of course, interfering, but I suppose I feared she would not have the nerve on her own.

The next evening, my last in California, I dined alone with the parents in a nearby restaurant. I broached the suggestion of the weekly lunch. The wife, naturally affectionate, and clearly fond of Amy, was doing her best to take the place of the dead mother, and I liked her.

Nothing was said for a moment. Jim looked at his wife, eyebrows up in question, but unsuspecting of the approaching squall.

"No," she said with finality. "No. It is out of the question." Her voice took a higher pitch. "I'm not going to be left alone, or shunted aside like that," and with that she burst into tears. Naturally, the subject was dropped like a hot frying pan, and I kicked myself for interfering in other people's lives. But Beth's good sense must have won out, because I heard, during the year that followed, that Amy and her father did enjoy a regular meal together on their own, with no harm done and no resentment on Beth's part. When at 19 Amy moved to a furnished room while attending college, her relationship with Beth and her father took a decided turn for the better. Here it had been Jim who had dug in his heels at the idea of his *baby* leaving home, and Beth who had helped her stepdaughter work it all out satisfactorily. Amy is now fond of them both, and considers them as a couple who belong together, not as her father taken over by a schemer. And she turns to Beth for advice, parental affection, and security.

The point is, I think, that the whole business of adults filling the role of parent to a child not their own is hazardous, filled with pitfalls, as rocky as a Vermont vegetable patch. Rational thought processes and controllable emotions can go by the board in a flash, leaving one resenting something, just *what* is hard to put a finger on, and feeling utterly silly and childish into the bargain. Resentment is part of the package in the step-relationship.

I have mentioned before that Andrew was often in hot water at school, and thus kept in Friday afternoons. This did not stop when his mother moved to California and he came to live with us full time. On the contrary, it continued with appalling regularity. But Noah found the school punishment inadequate and devised his own touch—the committing to memory of an assigned poem before the end of the weekend. The length of the poem depended upon the seriousness of the "crime."

One might well believe that this would poison

the boy's mind and heart against poetry altogether. Not a bit of it. He developed a facility for memorizing and a storehouse of poetic literature that was not only invaluable, but which spilled over onto the rest of us. I can still declaim parts of Drayton's "Fair stood the wind for France . . ." or "Onward they came and then . . ." from "The Charge of the Light Brigade," or ". . . did Kubla Khan/A stately pleasure dome decree/Where Alph . . ." Stuffily, my contribution to the choice of poem was Polonius' advice to Laertes (because I'd learned it in school, and could recite it myself).

While angry and resentful at the start of each memorizing exercise, by the time the poem had been conquered, Andrew was proud of his achievement (rightly so) and by the same token, Nick and Sam envious, both of his knowing it and hogging the stage while reciting it with appropriate gestures, and of the glamorous business of getting into trouble and having important and impressive punishments meted out to him. As for me, I yearned for Nick to be kept in, so that he too could lay away a treasure chest, a dowry, of familiar poems. Not a chance.

It is the fortunate person who is able to grab the nettle of adversity and turn it to advantage. This has always been Andrew's way. In later adolescence, when disappointed in love and moony sick about it, he buried himself in his books, and came out of it with prizes, commendations, and ultimately, naturally, a new girl.

    I remember a similar sort of experience in my own growing up—which, however, did not leave me with such a valuable residue, alas. I must have been 8 or 9 when my mother, frequently finding my bureau drawers a combination of ragbag odds and ends and magpie nest, would with regularity dump the whole drawer upside down on the floor and compound the whole higgledy-piggledy mess. Each time I would feel furious, unable to talk to her or anyone else. But in the course of putting everything back tidily, which took a good hour or more, I was enamored of the order of it all, and worked myself back into good humor again. I'd prefer a stock of poems to release at will from the caverns of my mind, however.

VIII

In one of my recent conversations with Andrew, he told me that life on the top floor of the Brooklyn house, the "children's floor," had been fun, and he thought they had all enjoyed it. I was delighted to hear it, and remembered with him the roughhousing, the meals at the round table in the kitchen with its view over Brooklyn rooftops, even the rules and routines. It was a pleasant change to reminisce nostalgically, instead of with our usual painful memories.

There can be little question that after eight years without brothers and then five days out of seven alone, the weekends with Nick and Sam, the pillow fights, untidy bathroom with water sloshing in and out of the tub, teethbrushing in concert, games and quizzes over the huge map of the United States Noah had tacked on the wall so that the boys would automatically absorb the shape of the states (Tennessee, for example, according to Andrew was in the shape of an eraser) and their capitals and relative positions, the freedom and the sense of being far away from censorious grown-ups, the lack of tension without me and his father—all of this was appealing and satisfying to Andrew at 9, 10, and 11. It was early on, he told me, that he and Nick began the welding of a relationship based on their mutual sense that it was them against the world. And it was then that the two of them would go off, saying they were visiting the "Pont," their refuge in time of trouble. I learned later that the Pont was a cafe on Pierre*pont* Street, and that they had only been there once, but had kept the name as a symbol when they had need of it.

    It is true that I too became aware of a solidarity between the two older boys, a sense that Noah and I (but particularly I) were enemies. While it made me uncomfortable, I didn't take it very seriously, and fortunately had enough sense to half realize that this was a natural aspect of the life of children, particularly male children, in their relationship with adults. It was in the way of a safety valve for the boys themselves. I had not read *Dream Days* and *The Golden Age* for nothing. Andrew today has more understanding of what that time meant to him than I did when it was actually taking place.

It was during these years that Noah began the slow process of teaching the boys about sex. What he was most interested in impressing on them was that they shouldn't fear it, feel it something to be ashamed about, something dirty that should be hidden, talked about in whispers. He encouraged rather free discussion, the telling of "dirty" stories (all pretty innocent, they were in fact), the learning of the words, the act, the processes. And they learned that masturbation was natural, indulged in by most males, and nothing for them to feel guilty about should they practice it.

I was grateful, for my own tendency was towards reticence and some discomfiture when sex was discussed or a bawdy story told. I was able to learn from this "schooling" also, for gradually my English self-consciousness lessened, my growing up as one of three sisters and consequent lack of frankness and openness about sex slowly overcome.

The summer before Andrew entered eighth grade, his mother moved to California, as I have already noted. She went because the conflict set up in Andrew and around him, placed as he was between two parents in disagreement, was too much for her and the boy to bear. It was tearing them both apart. So from that time on he visited her during the summer months, when she had him completely to herself, without unsettling weekends elsewhere and angry telephone conversations between his parents. He lived with us during the winter and was literally now a part of our household—in fact its kingpin. Superficially, at least, we all settled down in amity.

His parents separated, Andrew tells me now, during a time when he had tremendous need for an outlet to his feelings. He remembers his parents as having been very close sexually. What was between his father and myself was obviously something different in his eyes, certainly less comfortable for him, less natural, less palatable. He remembers how much he missed their "togetherness," and his feeling of being part of it.

His mother's leaving, in effect putting the entire country between them for most of the year, came, Andrew felt, when he was entering puberty and desperate for maternal affection, openly displayed. And so, in spite of the always latent wariness between us, he turned to me at this moment. And I rejected him. The impression that this left was a lasting one.

Andrew remembers clearly one evening, when I said goodnight as he lay in his bed. The other boys must have been at their father's, for he was alone. As I bent down to kiss him, he pulled me closer and was reluctant to let me go.

I remember quite clearly going into the front room on the top floor, the dark pool surrounding the bed, the whole lit only by the lamp in the street outside and that shadowed partly by a tree. I remember looking down at Andrew, his hazel eyes darker, but gleaming up at me, seeing the shine too of the blue and yellow striped linoleum with his slippers askew on it beside the bed, and the boy's half-smile that embarrassed me. I can sense again that wiry pajama-clad little body squirming close to me, the arms that wouldn't let me go. I don't think there was any calculation about this; he needed and wanted my closeness, my physical involvement with him. He was 13. I was embarrassed, and so I struggled and pulled to get out of his arms.

But I do not recall the sequel. I did not remember that he reached out his hands, as he says now, after I had straightened up, and clutched at my breasts, and that I'd backed sharply away, in shock.

"I don't know what to do, how to handle this," he remembers my saying. "I must see what your father will say."

It must have been more than a rejection—a betrayal as well. From this time on, he believes, stems his resentment and open antagonism; on that day he turned away from me altogether.

Of course I had felt some concern about the sexual content of our relationship, but really only academically. I don't think I applied it, or even knew how to. But it is an aspect that should be considered by stepparents with stepchildren of the opposite sex. To me now, it seems obvious that a spot of professional advice wouldn't have come amiss; I am less sure than I was that intelligence, common sense, and kindness are enough to pull one through. And as Andrew pointed out to me, the age of the stepchild vis-à-vis puberty and adolescence is crucial, one that provides the key to behavior—a key I was without.

In any case, Andrew turned at this time, for some sort of sexual outlet, to hear him tell it, to Nick, with whom he established a rapport that was something removed from their past comradeship and the brotherly affection I had hoped for. Andrew asked me, in this recent conversation, if I had been aware of this, had even thought about such a thing.

"No," I answered. "But children always play doctor or some such game, don't they?"

"That's not what I mean, at all," Andrew said, but he did not amplify, only went on to tell me that the relationship continued during part of the year, until the moment he kissed the younger boy on the mouth. Nick recoiled, ". . . and it was no longer the same; it was something he couldn't handle, and he retreated," Andrew explained. Here too is an aspect of the step-relationship that doesn't occur, at least very often, between brothers. Unless I'm even more naive than I think.

By this time dear Mrs. White was no longer with us, and I had turned to a Latin American employment agency for replacement. This took the shape of a slender, sulkily attractive divorcee of 28, with no English to speak of, lonely, no cultural or social resources, only anxious to make enough money to return to her southern homeland. Her name, astonishing as it turned out, was Modesta, and noting her ripeness, it was to her that Andrew turned next for his developing sexuality.

In theory, but only vaguely had I thought it through, I'd expressed aloud my belief that the old continental system of a father's taking his son to a whorehouse for initiation was rather a sensible solution to adolescent restlessness, incipient sexual curiosity and appetite. And I'd heard from time to time, from aunts and cousins, the tales of my grandmother's home in New York, where she had looked the other way when her five sons, as each grew towards maturity, were "serviced" by the maids of the household. I hadn't been particularly shocked, as I remember. Amused, perhaps.

In my own home, at my own hearth, I felt differently. There is still today not too far back in my mind's eye, the vivid outline of Modesta, framed in the doorway to her room, as I turned the curve of stairs to the top floor one evening after the boys' supper. Flushed, still damp, she had clearly just emerged from a bath (for want of anything else to do, doubtless), and leaned there, weight on one foot and hip out, draped by a bath towel that just managed to cover the crucial areas. She looked, I remember thinking, exactly like the cover of a current novel: *The Girl on the Via Flaminia.*

"Put something on, Modesta," I said inanely (it should be the title line in a song) and went downstairs again to think *that* one out. It was next day, when I had rather stumblingly tried to tell her it wasn't very wise to roam the top floor unclad around growing, healthy boys, that she turned the tables, she thought, by informing me Andrew had tried to assault her.

Since Andrew was small for 13, and though strong, not really a match for such a buxom adult as Modesta, I didn't take it that seriously. But I was myself confused as to how I really felt about it all, and hovered between some sense of responsibility towards the unhappy Modesta and outrage that even at 13 Andrew should ever force himself on anyone, and irritation at the girl's come-hither posture to the boy—a clear invitation in his eyes. He, of course, couldn't understand my criticism of *him* at all, since I had doubtless voiced my old theories in his presence at an earlier time. Having seen Modesta's perhaps unwitting (though I doubt it) attitude of invitation, I could hardly blame the boy. But theory is one thing, practice another, I discovered. I told Modesta I thought she'd be happier back home in South America. She agreed, and packed her suitcases without rancor.

Today Andrew tells me that she'd encouraged his "feeling her up," as he put it, all along, and even enjoyed it to the point of allowing younger brother Nick to share the fun, instructed the while by Andrew. Even 8-year-old Sam was shown how to cup his tiny hands around her ample bosom—a difficult matter, as he could hardly reach her unless she bent down. In any event, Andrew said, Sam could only roll on the floor in a fit of the giggles, he thought it all so funny—a joke in which Modesta joined, apparently.

Clearly, Andrew spiced life up for the other two boys.

Although we doubtless were saved some even more complicated problems in terms of the step-relationships, not having daughters, I think it might have made life easier for the boys, and they would have had a more natural attitude towards girls, had this not been the case. They all felt a bit self-conscious and ill at ease in female company, Andrew in particular, to the point of throwing up with excitement when he was asked out to parties or at the thought of taking a girl for a soda or the movies. To counter this, we enrolled all three boys in Miss Hepburn's dancing class at Grace Church, a fixture in Brooklyn Heights for decades. All three of them wore the required white gloves, and learned how to see their partner back to her seat and leave her with a slight bow, how to go through the motions of accepted party politeness, and above all, how to dance well.

Nevertheless it was an uncomfortable situation, without any free and easy give and take between the sexes. A sister who brought her friends to the house would have changed the scene. Nick and Sam did have a half-sister on Long Island; perhaps that is why they had a bit less trouble in feeling at ease with girls.

Recently Sam told me that he thought all three of them suffered very much, in their attempts at some sort of relationship with girls. Nick probably had the easiest time of it, he thought. I believe, if this is so, it is due to his attending the coeducational Brooklyn Friends School until he was 14. Andrew spent no schooldays with girls after the second grade, Sam after fourth, until college. The product of a city boys' school, who has no sisters, whose family does not belong to a country or social club of some sort where he can meet girls, experiences a very stilted and self-conscious sort of relationship with the other sex. Boys and girls meet at dancing school, at Parents' League parties, or at the subscription parties and dances during the holiday season—and none of these do much to put gangly, awkward teenagers at ease with each other.

    This chapter seems to be more concerned with Andrew than the others, and it includes his adventures with girls. This may be because he was a boy who talked to us about everything he did. He had no reticence, and since he'd been trained to describe everything he did, and did it well, for a long time he had a willing audience. The other boys were clams by comparison. Andrew also accepted little on faith—a good trait for the searching scholar, but one that gave problems while he was growing up. It was easy enough to steer Nick and Sam into acceptance of a belief in, for example, my sense of values towards parents, women, adults, or other people in general. I'd say possibly this even led to too much concern for the welfare and opinion of others. It was really no hardship for them to refrain from using four-letter words in front of me—and thus not have the need either to say them in public generally. Andrew enjoyed articulating them, their shock effect and how they made him feel, and he used them. I could tell Nick and Sam that I didn't like something, and they'd accept my judgment, even if they didn't particularly agree or understand. It isn't that they were spineless, either. It was just not worth bickering about trivialities, and besides they wanted to learn.

Andrew questioned everything. If he disagreed, he argued. If he didn't understand, he showed his feelings by an openly reluctant compliance. With all of the boys, I tried to utilize prevention; if I saw a problem that might arise, I thought about how to deal with it ahead of time. This kind of thinking was unlikely to work with Andrew, and if Noah thought I was on the boy's back too much, he wouldn't listen either. I stopped trying; to them, I was a worrywart—how did I know things would turn out that way, perhaps they wouldn't, so forget it. During Andrew's late teens, however, he did begin to consult me about girls, and sometimes other matters; and he began to listen to what I told him. At least, I *think* he did.

Andrew fell in love for the first time with a thud—with the daughter of one of my father's academic friends. The boy was in Princeton one day, visiting. When this bouncy, button-nosed and forget-me-not-eyed miss entered the dusty book-lined scriptorium where my father worked, Andrew was immediately smitten. Poppy was a gay pixie with a pony tail. She had been conventionally brought up, and Andrew was a new animal to her, a very exciting one. Throughout the spring of the year they were together whenever possible. Correspondence was hot and heavy. Poppy was a serious girl as well, and a good student. A year younger than Andrew, she was entranced by his quick mind, the books he'd read, his curiosity, his offbeat experiences. But she was frightened by the boy's singleminded intensity and by her own emotions, and she was troubled at her inability to reconcile her upbringing and her desires. Rather typically, they were two adolescents in love for the first time.

When Andrew had told us of his going to a "cat house," as he called it with grown-up nonchalance, while he was in Aruba (this was during the summer he spent working as an apprentice oiler on a tanker) when his ship docked there overnight, our reaction was one of amusement and perhaps suppressed worry lest he had caught anything. He described to us the evening with the whore, whom his shipmates had urged him to visit, and of course traditionally he'd convinced himself he could help her, perhaps even rehabilitate her. We listened, nodded sagely, and thought no more about it.

But nothing in Poppy's background—more nineteenth than mid-twentieth century—had prepared her for this particular experience in a young man's life. As with most adolescents, basic honesty and need to "tell everything" to his love compelled him to recount the story to Poppy; maybe he wanted to boast a bit. It was a mistake. She did not know how to handle the information, but she *did* know she was bothered by it. Her previous suspicion that perhaps she was too young for this sort of intense relationship was reinforced, however, by Andrew's disclosure. Unhappily she wrote him at school that they'd better not continue to see each other, and that this was her last letter to him. After this blow, Andrew played the field for some time.

In general, I reacted to Andrew's *affairs* (as that first relationship was not) with girls before his college days much, I suppose, as I would have if he'd been my natural son—chiefly with a belief that it was his business, not mine, but also with interest and perhaps amusement, and counsel when he wanted it. He often did. Here, there was a difference between him and the other two, who rarely asked my opinion, one way or the other, as regards their girls. What was different, too, was the fact that he told us so much. Naturally, I felt a bit uncomfortable when the subject of one of his narratives came to the house. But the situation didn't become anything I wanted to make an issue out of until he went to France in the summer between school and college, working in Paris and managing on the pittance it paid him.

Paris to an 18-year-old was all it should have been, and he made the most of it, absorbing the light-filled paintings at the Jeu de Paume, the tingling brilliance of the Étoile at night, the visits to bôites with his boss and the visiting Tom Mboya, the chestnut trees, Montmartre, living on fruit, bread, cheese, pâté and wine, and above all the freedom of being on his own for the first time in his life.

In the beginning he stayed in a too chaperoned pension found for him by his office. Then at a Chinese hotel, no less, on the Left Bank. It was filled with students, many of them foreigners like himself. And the letters we received that summer were graphic in the details of Andrew's amorous experiences with the various girls who sequentially shared his room. I squirmed. Noah, after his initial vicarious enjoyment of the pleasures of Paris at 18, which he'd not been lucky enough to have himself, became uncomfortable as well, though he wouldn't admit it. I read Andrew's letters in silence from then on. At a certain point I told Noah I planned to speak to the boy of the need for reticence in sexual matters, that 18 meant manhood and private lives, not to be bruited about or shared with those not involved. Mumbling a bit, he agreed.

And when I did just that, on his return to America, Andrew was pleasant, even interested and consenting (not that this lack of reticence disappeared overnight). He had developed, over the last year or so, a way of convincing me that he believed I knew what I was talking about, that my instincts and values were the right ones, and that he trusted me in this, and would try to abide by my precepts, even though he didn't always agree or even understand what I was driving at. He was growing up. And by this time he knew me—possibly far better than I knew him. He was learning to take advantage of what I could do for him, as well as to keep from me that part of his existence about which we would certainly disagree. When I saw this to be so, I was proud. And I was relieved that we seemed to be working out our relationship, molding it into something viable and valuable to us both. Perhaps everything would be smooth sailing from now on (the reader who has come this far will know better than I did then how ludicrous such an idea was!).

I think all parents are wise who work out together how they feel and think and wish to deal with certain problems sure to arise as their children grow into adolescence and mature into adulthood. Mores and ethical outlooks can be worked out, or if not, talked out so that at the critical moment the parents are not lost or morassed in shock as they discover they disagree. They will know ahead of time each other's way of looking at each question. Problems can be discussed, before confrontations with children over dates, hours, habits, and so on rise up to bewilder them.

For stepparents, it is even more important to obviate the possibility of friction, of presenting division instead of a united front. Realistically, unhappily, this rarely happens. At least, it didn't with us. I had taken no stance one way or the other about the boys' sleeping with a girl while we were all cozily at rest under the same roof. I hadn't even contemplated such a thing, and hadn't brought the matter up for discussion. But one night I woke up and went into the living room, only to see Andrew turning the handle of the guest room door. He was 19, and it was 2:00 A.M.

I was thoroughly discomfited, but I slunk back to bed without being seen. It was I who had written to Elsa's mother the week before, inviting her to stay. At the first opportunity to see Andrew alone, I told him quite simply and with utter conviction that this was not to happen again.

"Okay," was all he said, with a completely straight face. It was all there was time for. Later I tried to explain myself. I could understand why the boys called it hypocritical for me to tell them, "What I don't know won't hurt me," when I am out of the house; it was hard to explain my position. But there were things involved in what had happened that weekend that I *could* explain. And I think Andrew found my reasoning valid, when I said that in writing to the girl's mother I was making myself responsible for her to her mother. "Being responsible" certainly didn't include the servicing of my son—or my stepson. Also, there was the matter of taste. Taste and good manners—these are not only hard to define and convey, they come close to intruding on that area young people now mark off as the hypocrisies of the middle-aged. I also touched upon the possible discomfort of the girl—for I did try to interpret the feminine viewpoint about matters to the boys because I think it differs from the male viewpoint. Whatever I conveyed to Andrew, in any case, I was undoubtedly firm enough to make my main point "never again."

Although the other two boys at first must have licked their lips in vicarious schoolboy delight at the details of Andrew's sexual adventures, I think they too became uncomfortable. In any event, there was little of that sort of "sharing" on their part. The closest I came with Nick was learning about the hair-raising escapes he had climbing out of Vassar and Wellesley dormitory windows in the middle of the night. The danger of expulsion or suspension from college wasn't any more agreeable to think about than Andrew's more explicit word pictures. With the younger boys, my experience was more that of trying to shush Noah when he asked if they had a girl these days, and if they were getting enough of it.

In this whole area of sex, the relationship between stepmother and stepson is perhaps easier and more meaningful than with natural children. Sons rarely consult their mother about such matters, the blood tie making for more embarrassment, somehow, than that between stepmother and stepson—for the stepmother is an outsider, really. (This can, of course, be turned to advantage.) But I firmly believe a parent is a parent, step or otherwise, who will and must stick to his own beliefs, whether ethical, moral, or anything else. If this breaks up a beautiful friendship between him and his children, it is too bad, but it cannot be helped. Again, to me, this is what helps a child grow up, deciding and choosing between his own beliefs and those of his parents. If there are no guidelines, no rules set and more or less adhered to, how can he make a choice? As is obvious, I was not, nor am I now, a permissive parent.

IX

We have all read the books or heard the lectures on radio and TV describing Momism in America. I believe we have even taken to heart the advice that the father of a family should have a positive, assertive, well-defined role in that family, a place that should not be taken over by his efficient executive-type wife. When there are children of different parents in that family and the blood father is not living with his children, as in Nick and Sam's situation, it is even more important, I think, that the household is not mother-dominated —beyond the inescapable fact that mother does control most of the family concerns involving the children's day-to-day existence. I don't really think it matters too much whether what the father does or says is right or wrong, just so he isn't always overruled, and just so he is a male figure on whom the boy child can pattern himself, who can protect his son when he needs it, encourage his male rowdiness in the face of his mother's pleas and generally encourage his son's male aggressiveness, just as he encourages his daughter's display of feminine daintiness and tastes and emulation of her mother. It isn't even too important, in my opinion, whether he is adored or disliked (the former is the more likely, when the children are little). It does matter if he isn't respected, if his word is disregarded, or if he always says, "Ask your mother," and lets her make the decisions. Obviously, it is equally bad if he is cruel and overbearing and a bully.

    Children will be bewildered by the disruption of their lives following their parents' separation and ultimate divorce. Their father has gone away, and there is no male in the house. Their mother seems irritable to them, perhaps unhappy. Therefore, if she remarries and a masculine figure is once more a part of the household, their existence takes a turn for the better. It will have improved even more, as I have pointed out, if this male doesn't have a way of passing the buck to his stepchildren's mother if he lacks confidence in his own opinions and precepts. Better by far, even if unpalatable, that he attempt to verbalize his attitudes and reactions and give to stepson or stepdaughter his own particular masculine viewpoint. The importance of the father or stepfather cannot, in my view, be minimized in a family where there are children.

I certainly had little worry on this score. Noah took stands, all right, and boy, did he have definite opinions! No one could ever maintain that he was a Milquetoast type of character, or that he was uxoriated—although to this day he likes to pretend he is. He set standards for his children, some good, some bad (one is never satisfied). I was overconcerned a lot of the time that he was being unfair, disinterested, insensitive (yes, even to Andrew), brusque, too much the perfectionist who asks the impossible of people, thus setting up fears of failure or inadequacy.

I don't think Nick held any of this against him. Sam certainly didn't. In fact, they resented him and his attitudes and actions or his lacks far less than they did my tentative motions on their behalf or my attempts to change my husband. I don't mean that they adored him either, but his superficial behavior towards them wasn't half as important as it was to me. They were more sensible than I, more realistic. If they had been girls, it would doubtless have been different. Girls can worry throughout the day over a cross word or an impatient look.

A friend of mine with two daughters, aged 10 and 13, has told me of her remarriage; these two rascals would plot half the night over the deviltry they were going to subject their stepfather to, the next day. But I don't believe there exists a cruel stepfather myth, or even one folk tale in which the stepfather mistreats his stepchildren. At least I haven't been able to find any, unless we include Claudius in *Hamlet*.

Perhaps this book should be called *Life With Father No. Two*. My husband was a definite personality—in the way a porcupine is, with no other creature of field or forest anything like him. He was prickly, yes, but could sheath his quills too, and be far more patient and tolerant than I. He expected certain things of the boys, certain behavior, an interest in and involvement with their own world of school and family, but also in the larger national and international world as well, and he helped them learn about it. Conversely, he was openly (sometimes to the point of cruelty) contemptuous of stupidity, lazy thinking, and acceptance of clichés. He held to values and standards that I believed in myself. Yes, all these demands put pressures on them that sometimes were too much, which they kicked against more and more as they grew up. But surely that is what growing up is all about. I made the mistake of thinking that the step-relationships in our family made things different, as though we had one pot to stir for Andrew, and another for Nick and Sam. That one shouldn't be so strict, hold such exacting standards because the little dears, deprived of their real father and the familiar pattern they had been used to, needed gentler treatment (and how about Andrew, who was also deprived, but of his mother when he was with us?). By my diffident suggestions to Noah that he be a little softer with them, by my half-baked criticism of him over injured feelings that I attributed to the boys but that were really my own, I could, I suppose, have emasculated him. Luckily, I was not forceful about it since I was unsure of myself. I buttoned my lip after one or two occasions when I glimpsed his hesitation and noted his unsureness, which made me realize my foolishness.

Of course, there is nothing very new about the see-sawing of parental roles. It happens in families without any kind of stepchildren complications. The point is, if a strong male figure is important in "normal" situations, clearly it is even more so when the structure of children's lives is made difficult and complex for them by a parent's remarriage.

During the years in Brooklyn, our weekend pattern was the way it was because Noah *was* the dominant male. We all did what he wanted, what he ordered. Not necessarily because we agreed, desired the same thing, or thought it right—but because opposition all too often made things unbearably difficult and upsetting. At least for me. Differences were compounded, I think now, because Noah and Andrew welcomed conflict often as though it was a game. I, and Nick as well, fled from it whenever possible. We just weren't capable of playing it their way. Nicky was better able to sidestep it and forget it. I tried to change them. The result was that I was unhappy and apprehensive.

    I tried to explain to Noah how I felt, using what I thought were rational arguments but which all too soon became overpowered by emotion. I was not very convincing as a rule. He would laugh, brush me off, or even fail to hear my too soft because unsurely spoken words. And so I'd resort to different tactics and write a well-worded, logically thought out, and I hoped objective argument on paper folded up into a *billet doux,* and lay it carefully with his wallet and loose change in the top drawer of his bureau. He did read these "love and hate" letters, and did take the points I made seriously. Until next time. It availed me little, and it didn't matter very much. Not that I thought so at the time, of course.

    But when he wanted to, and this was more

often than it may have appeared in this account of our life together, Noah made all our lives rather wildly interesting. This is what mattered. He had imagination, tremendous nervous energy, and wild kooky ideas. Many of the things he did with us, or had done before and told us about, were scary and adventurous. We probably wouldn't have done them ourselves, but he made them exciting and somehow acceptable.

    Nick and Sam sat with mouths agape when I described my first date with Noah. First of all, it was winter and we were going to Montauk Point! He had borrowed a car and parked it, while he came in for me, on one of the little side streets running north and south, parallel to Riverside Drive. Instead of driving in the same direction until we reached an intersection, he calmly drove over the grass island and swung back down into the southern lane of the Drive. The car rocked wildly. It took a good ten blocks for me to recover.

    At a later time Sam told me of a similar incident, when he and Noah drove uptown one afternoon in search of a music stand. The sidewalk in front of the shop was, unkindly, adjacent to a Tow Away zone. That is where Noah parked. Sam was fearful, verging on being upset. "Live dangerously, boy," Noah told him, putting his arm across his shoulders and drawing him into the store.

In Brooklyn one fine weekend, the four of them, Noah, Andrew, Nick and Sam, spent hours clambering in and out of waterfront warehouses and through empty buildings awaiting the wreckers' iron ball. One evening as dusk was falling the boys burst into the house, with Noah sedately bringing up the rear. In their arms was a whole batch of ceramic tiles, beautiful and ancient-looking in spite of the grime and mortar covering them, that they had pried loose from around some nineteenth-century fireplace. They gave them to me as an offering, joyously, and I reacted like a mother.

"They don't belong to us," I protested. But my moralistic reception didn't stop me from accepting them all in the end. The tiles were quite extraordinary, colored in mellow browns, tans, and yellows. Some I used for gifts. The rest, carefully carried with me each time I moved, now sit snugly cemented into my present kitchen wall.

I'll never forget the trip Noah and I took with Sam up into New England. Our friends the Tabors and daughter Nancy, Sam's age, came along as well. We stopped for dinner one evening at a country inn written up in guide books and staffed, that time of year, with dollar-hungry college kids. We were still sitting around an empty table, famished and waiting for a glimpse of the menu, when one of these young boys placed a tray under Noah's nose. On it were three ten dollar bills, and some loose change. My husband calmly swept the money from the tray and turned to Ben Tabor. "You got two bucks for the tip, Ben?" he asked without cracking a smile. They had been friends since college, and Ben's turn of humor matched Noah's. "Sure," he answered, and with great deliberation put down two single dollar bills on the tray. The waiter said thank you, and turned away. Some time later he returned, after some irate diner demanded his change. Everything was straightened out satisfactorily. We even ate. During maneuvers, Sam and Nancy hadn't known which way to look. They were astonished. They were embarrassed. Then they broke up.

    These adventures, besides being fun even if startling, had the side benefit of teaching the boys to use their own judgment about what was responsible behavior and what not, to say no sometimes when Noah suggested an escapade (sometimes just to see what their reaction would be, let me say) that was utterly outlandish. Since I was the sissy and the moralist, we gave them a pretty balanced picture by the exaggerated attitudes held by us both—eventually they would be able to choose for themselves. Today they are not prudes, they are not prissy, they are not scaredycats. They are idealists, yes, but pretty realistic ones. I don't think either Noah or I passed on to any one of the three boys our rosy-colored spectacles.

During his scholarship-supported college days (and therefore under an assumed name) Noah had played semipro baseball, in spite of the fact that even then his interests were intellectual in the extreme. And so he loved to toss a ball with the boys and, whenever he could, took them to watch Dodger or even Yankee games.

One of his more whimsical touches was giving to people and inanimate objects odd handles and personalities and he introduced Nick and Sam to this particular amusement. Andy already shared it. Noah was clever at catching some half-hidden, secret aspect of appearances. There were always our friends in the water pipes, who had traveled down to Brooklyn when we all did (Andrew thought they had lived there all along): Oski Moffy Shvoo Shvoo and Nopki Walli. Sam calls Noah *Oski* on occasion to this day. The first thing Noah told the boys on their arrival in the Brooklyn house, fresh from summer camp, were the names of the two black lamps with elongated Modigliani faces. Piero and Francesca, he said, would talk across the room to each other after everyone had gone to bed. "Come down and listen, some night," Noah suggested.

Nick and Sam's Uncle Bob, or second cousin really, he of the pale blue eyes and large ears and who scuttled from place to place in half run, half walk, was of course the White Rabbit. Noah's aunt, whom they soon met, was the Robin, for obvious reasons. Sam became Sam'l Squirl the Money Man, because he had a way of squirreling away the nickles and dimes he was given as though they were nuts for winter consumption, and he always had a store of them to draw upon—very much in the way I used to hoard my melting ice cream cone, so that when everyone else had finished, I was still happily licking away. Sam enjoyed his name so much he still signs his name Squirl in letters to us, in spite of his 5'11" frame and rather assertive manner. I was—and still am—Zuzu, usually shortened to Zu, because I once put a small box of Nabisco Zuzu gingersnaps in Noah's bed.

As I said before, there is no cruel stepfather myth. A man, by the nature of his maleness, has an easier time of it with stepchildren. He is not prone to worry, to wonder if they love him or like him, or whether he cares about them, or if he did the right or wrong thing. He accepts people and situations as they are. I realize generalizations are a pitfall; a man with stepdaughters doubtless has problems galore, but they still don't trouble him as much and as persistently. I believe a woman worries more, by *her* nature, is more sensitive to feelings, nuances, subtleties, that don't bother a man at all—and shouldn't.

Of course fathers see their role differently. Martin, my first husband, had another attitude about child rearing, or at least towards the handling of his sons now living somewhere else. While Nick and Sam were growing up, he was governed by the principle of removing pressure from them as much as he possibly could. He was there, yes, if they sought him out, if they needed him. But they lived with their mother and *her* husband, and this husband was really the man in their lives most of the time. Martin was not about to set up any sort of competition with this man that could be troublesome for his sons to cope with. They had one family environment, and it was in Brooklyn. He was not going to pull them every which way by insisting they were part of his family too (of course it was easier for him to do this because he had a new wife and three children who were not anyone's stepchildren, in his second family). However, I didn't have any sense that he made Nick and Sam feel, either, that they did not belong in this other family when they were there. Perhaps he realized, whether on a conscious level or not I don't know, that two Clarence Day fathers would be a bit too Sisyphean for small boys. Anyway, when they visited him on Long Island, the weekend was all on a lower key, without conflict to speak of and therefore calming and safe. Above all, there was no competition. That the two boys might believe their father not to be too interested in them was a danger he risked, of course. But not one that could not be set right—and was, I believe, later on when they were older.

Noah operated on an entirely different tack with Andrew, influenced not only by his own temperament, beliefs, and compulsions, but by the fact that his ex-wife did not remarry. Andrew clearly needed a strong and assertive masculine figure in his life, and by God he, Noah, was going to provide that figure.

Each father played a valid role vis-à-vis his sons, while each was rather at the extreme of the range of possibilities. Both attitudes were to be respected, and did more good than harm to the boys.

A current novelist has written that he was

being forced to divorce his kid as well as his wife. Noah certain did *not,* one of the lucky few among men in his position. Of course he played the same robust role with Sam and Nick also, without any soul-searching about its being good or bad for them. He was natural, and acted as spontaneously with them as he did with other people. Although he was an intellectual and highly introspective person, somehow these qualities didn't spill over so much that they inhibited his actions.

Having no difficulty about verbalizing his opinions, his reactions, his attitudes, Noah wanted Andrew to develop the same skill. He was highly articulate (I sometimes think too much so, and Andrew too), and while his son even at that time gave every sign of having inherited this talent, or characteristic, Noah made sure of it by training him and developing it (he tried to do the same for me, but I resisted, wanting to keep on telling my husband what happened in my own rather scatter-brained and haphazard way).

"What are you reading, Andy?" he would say. "What is it about? Tell me the story." Or "What happened at the ball game today?" or "How did the outing with Mr. Gillespie go today, did you get into trouble?" He would question him endlessly, weekends before he was with us all the time, about school that day, happenings during the week, what he had done with his mother, the people he'd seen, TV programs he'd looked at. And Andrew was an apt pupil. He learned to play this game well, to make a story out of everything, a good one with a beginning, a middle, and an end. He learned to infect his narrative with drama, with his own zest about everything, so that his hearers were caught up in his enthusiasm. Obviously, this helped to make him the excellent teacher I believe he is today (and I have sat in on his classes and seen him at work).

Noah attempted the same workout with Nick with less immediate success. Nick was a more deliberate, even deeper, thinker and speaker, less verbal by nature than Andrew, and far more thoughtful. Noah could barely restrain his impatience at the "ums," and "You know's" and other forms of gaining time. Yet Nick did learn, too. When he in turn went away to boarding school, he could come home and tell us about the happenings that interested him or that he thought might interest us; he too began to develop the capacity of launching into an orderly and systematic account. It is naturally a question whether he would have become more articulate without this sort of pressure put on him, just by virtue of his own intellectual development and training at school.

Sam was not really as much the object of this systematic training as the other boys had been. But naturally he wanted to emulate his brothers, and attempted the same sort of organized narrative from an early age. And now he is as adept at it as the others. The boys were really conditioned by this. Successful at it or not, when they reached home and Noah and I were in the living room, they would almost automatically sit themselves down and begin. It is amusing, now that I look back on it. And even then, it was a useful tool that Noah was developing in the boys. Each adapted it to his own particular ways and talents, and I realized this and appreciated it. Andrew's style was at first exaggerated, histrionic, spilling out details of his own and others' experiences almost ad nauseam until he learned restraint; Nick was diffident, and reticent to a fault, playing his whole life pretty close to his chest, but finally learning to share some of it, in a slightly cool, philosophical way that hid the eagerness underneath. Sam bubbles and infects us all with his involvement in what he is doing, with his *joie de vivre*.

Of course, a stepfather's empathy and sensitivity to his stepchildren can make all the difference to their lives and that of their mother—that is, their lives from 7:30 in the morning to whenever they go to bed. With all these complicated relationships every member of the home is highly sensitized if not sensitive (unhappily, I was both to an inordinate degree). A man, as I have said, is less likely to be sensitive about the rights and wrongs of his day-to-day relationships—even to the dignity and feelings of young children. Noah, certainly, was more attuned to Andrew than anyone else he knew, because he was his own son. He felt guilty towards the boy; and he had him buried deep in his own gut. But even with Andrew, he made mistakes. For example, Noah questioned him not only regularly, but in public, as to his behavior during the week (when he lived weekdays with his mother). He was scolded in front of others, and even his punishments took on the aura of public entertainment—I must say Andrew himself helped to make this so, as he would far rather we were all involved around him, even unpleasantly, than around someone else. And I say entertainment in the way some sensitive Romans might have viewed the encounter between Christians and lions, for I don't think the boys enjoyed it much, and I certainly didn't.

When Noah came home in the evening, he always asked me how things had gone during the day. And because Andrew was always in his mind and on his conscience in that full year before boarding school that Andrew lived in Brooklyn, the first thing he'd say would be: "How's Andrew? Was he all right today? Did he give you any trouble? And how about Modesta, any complaints?"

In the beginning, I was so bewildered at my new and too complicated life, at my sudden ineptitude in dealing with small boys when before I'd felt no uncertainty, that I would fall in with these queries and tell my husband what *had* happened during the day—usually none of it good. Then Noah would tax Andrew with it all, be angry with him, and unreasonably, but so humanly, angry with me as well. This is an unbearable situation for father, son, and stepmother. The stepmother must learn to deal with all minor transgressions on her own. I mean all, even if she needs and yearns for a sympathetic ear or a comforting word. She only makes more heartache for herself if she doesn't—as I did, for it took me a long time to understand why my husband included me in his wrath and even longer, if ever, not to mind about it.

Nevertheless, and I have proved it, father, children, stepchildren, and stepmother, given good will, energy, and a stout heart, can and will live through it all without being destroyed in the process. At least, that is how it turned out with us. Although poor Andy. What he needed was objectivity from me, serenity, patience, kindness, open arms, and more than a dash of intelligent understanding. He didn't receive many of them at the same time, and so he didn't know quite how to behave himself, and was torn in pieces by his guilt—until he got away from all of us and went to boarding school.

Noah was in an impossible position, if one thinks about it. Most fathers who are part of this sort of family equation cannot avoid being so. Much as he loved his son and suffered profound guilt at what he had done to him by his divorce, he also loved his new wife, whom he realized only too well he was subjecting to unhappiness and worry because of his son's behavior and disruptive effect. He told himself that he loved his stepsons— and he was undoubtedly genuinely fond of them— but he could not have been human had he not been annoyed sometimes or even envious that they were well behaved, seemingly uncomplicated little animals without obvious neuroses or problems with which he had to deal.

The close relationship between Andrew and Noah was the pivotal pole of the circus tent under which we all lived. It is true that as he grew older, Andrew had to learn to discriminate between his own tastes, his own values, and those of his father's, with whom he had identified so completely for so long. For many years Noah was Andrew's oracle, and his favored companion whenever possible. And Noah, for his part, was absorbed in the boy, in the way his mind worked, in his likes and dislikes, his conscious and unconscious, his actions and reactions.

And so when the three boys were together, the contrast between his preoccupation with his son and his feelings about the other boys was evident; to me it appeared as thinly disguised indifference to them. Today I don't think it was—only because of the intensity of the other involvement did it seem so. If it wasn't as obvious as I believed, there was my fear that sooner or later it would be made clear to the younger boys. And the other side of the same coin was my feeling that this sort of concentrated attention surrounding one young boy could not possibly be good for him, and had perhaps something to do with his evident need to be the star performer, for praise or blame—either one would do.

Of course, Noah was not indifferent. Where the mistake lay, it seems to me, was in his telling himself and them, and me, and the world that he had three sons who were all treated alike. He didn't have three sons, he had one, and he did treat him differently, willy-nilly, from his two stepsons, because he loved him as a son. He could love the others, and I think he grew to love them (at first he loved them, in a sense, because they were part of me), but *not* as sons.

They had a father already, who felt them in *his* gut, even if not to the same extent (after all, he was blessed with more than one child, five to be exact, and so his feelings and interest did not have to be funneled into one bottlemouth, but could rather be dispersed).

Both fathers, during those first years anyway, saw their sons for short periods at a time. Of course, everyone's behavior is going to be strained, unnatural, and at a higher pitch of feeling under such circumstances. But I didn't remember this, or use it to comfort me when I felt hurt for the sake of my sons. It was foolish. So again, I say—to knock the nail on the head once more—a stepchild is not the same as a child, a stepson is not the same as a son, a stepdaughter is not the same as a daughter. A father or a mother of course loves his or her child more, cannot help but be more involved in him and his doings. So stepmothers, don't be hurt, don't be resentful, don't take things personally.

Nick and Sam were not damaged by the lesser intensity of their relationship with Noah (it could even be argued that they were better off without it). There was the good strong father figure when they needed him, who did not involve them in feelings of guilt, shame, and so forth for how they felt about him. They had no doubts about where he stood—foursquare behind them—if any serious crisis befell them, if they were in trouble and needed him. And in some ways they were able to mature more easily and more naturally than Andrew, who for so long depended on his father for counsel, advice, and orders—to the point that he was lazy or timid about making his own decisions.

Noah believed in chores for boys, while himself being more the European intellectual man of the house, unable to hammer a nail and not wishing to learn, unwilling to wash or dry a dish—to say nothing of barbecuing a steak. That was to be strictly my department. This made it hard to instill in the boys an acceptance of the duties we both, as parents, felt should be part of the home educative process. And we not only wanted them to carry out their jobs but to do them with responsibility and grace.

Cindy the puli was my job, though Sam, as he grew bigger and stronger, did take her on some of the time—when the older boys were already away at school. When Andrew left for Hotchkiss, the garbage duty fell to Nick. Many a time did I have to cope with: "God dammit, why hasn't Nick put the pails out?" or "Damn Nick, there's a lid on the sidewalk, and the pails haven't been taken in. What's the matter with him?"

Noah also believed in neatness and cleanliness —in blue buttondowns, polished loafers, and crew-cut hair (which looked fine atop Noah's and Andrew's bony features but was less flattering to Nick and Sam's squarer faces). This was fine when the boys were little, and I, similarly old-fashioned with English-trained ideas, glowed quietly at the sight of the three angels at our huge annual Christmas party, hair slicked, navy blue blazers and gray flannels well creased, and faces ashine. This was good training for the prep schools all attended at a later date.

But Brooklyn Friends School was relaxed about such things, and besides, Brooklyn wasn't Manhattan, I tried to explain. Nick suffered rather obviously from Noah's preferences, and even openly rebelled, though he took in silence Noah's unthinkingly disparaging comments about his friend Dan's pink, tab-collared shirt, pointed blue suede shoes, and wide leather belt over hip-hugging jeans.

In spite of, or because of, the difference in intensity of feeling between stepparents and their stepchildren, it is a pity that everyone cannot be relaxed about such minor things as clothes and hair styles. I found Dan to be a pleasant and kind boy, gentle and intelligent. Far easier to deal with, for me, than Andrew's rambunctious fellow students at Collegiate, for all their Oxford shirts and navy blazers. It wasn't only the style of dress at Friends that Noah abhorred. Perhaps the unhappy year Andrew had spent there in constant friction with his rather limited second grade teacher, before Noah and I were married, had something to do with it. He didn't say so, however, but was verbal in his contempt for the school's curriculum of civics, social studies and linguistics, as compared with the traditional Latin, mathematics and foreign languages typifying the studies at Collegiate. And so Noah put Nick's school down, along with the boy himself (though unaware he was doing so, of course). I don't think this would have been the case had Nick been his natural son—or, as is likely, he'd have had the same opinions but taken far more pains to conceal them.

The situation was paralleled, more or less, when Sam, thought to be not strong enough for the austere rigors of Hotchkiss, went to Gunnery, again a smaller, more permissive, and less exacting sort of school.

Surely a man must feel, and therefore bury, some sort of jealousy in his attitude to his new wife's son by a former marriage—the rather obvious sign of a sexual relationship in which he had no part. Add to this his recognition of his stepson's good qualities—sweetness, responsibility, and also the much vaunted intellectuality—and his own son's troublemaking propensities; underneath he is bound to harbor some sort of rancor, concealed or overt.

I remember vividly one occasion when this rancor, or even jealousy, flared into the open. Noah was at that time a regular lecturer to a weekend seminar for company executives, and this particular weekend we all went along, since it took place at a country club where there was tennis, swimming, and golf to amuse the boys and keep them occupied while Noah was working or he and I were socializing. One afternoon Noah and I played nine holes of golf, which we liked to do on the few occasions we were close to a course. We took Nick with us, since he was soon going to Hotchkiss where he could play golf on his own. He was 13 and for him rather openly at odds with us. But his rebellion was quiet, and he did not make trouble for anyone else, just hugged it all close to his chest. On this particular afternoon, he had no wish to play, or be with us. We insisted, having gone to the trouble of buying left-handed clubs for him to take to school and having brought them with us for the weekend (of such petty matters do parents' irritation with offspring stem). We set out, the three of us, and we all played a lousy game. Nick couldn't even hit the ball, and cared less. Noah sliced and hooked and fumed at the lot of us. And I fluttered.

Back in our hotel room I stupidly gave some indication that Nick's behavior had upset me (when I think back to all the times Andrew had done this, I have to smile). With no further ado, Noah went next door to the boys' room and called him in. My husband strenuously denies ever saying these words, but say them he did in the heat of his fury: "If you upset your mother like that again, Nicholas, I'll *kill* you."

Jealousy of any kind is ugly, embarrassing and a puzzle to those it touches, and insoluble. It certainly makes for trouble between husband and wife, but it is, I think, not only without solution but unavoidable. The trick is not to be oversensitive or hurt when it rears its ugly head. Children do survive. Ours would too, with all that we had going for them. While I floundered in the whirlpool of personalities in my family, most of the time I hadn't the sense, or view-from-a-distance ability to realize that there were some pretty strong bonds welding it together. That the boys were attached to one another, did esteem each other for their very real and valuable qualities, did accord us respect and obey us, and did find some consolation for the schizoid quality of their home life in each other's companionship, all made for heartwarming solidarity in a crisis.

It happened during the year Andrew spent under the Brooklyn roof. Our house was heated by oil, fed into it through a huge rubber hose by Paragon once each winter month. The burner was in the basement hall, near the playroom and TV set. It was old, renovated, and had various quirks, one of them being the need to empty rusty water out of a gauge every so often. Noah was doing this one evening after supper. The boys were up on the top floor, while I was washing the dishes in our minuscule kitchen off the living room.

Suddenly we heard a shout, loud, with a controlled but definite sense of urgency. "Andy! Nick! Come here at once. Down in the basement. Hurry!"

The two older boys were there in what Noah told me later seemed like one jump, and I right behind them, with red-cheeked little Sammy bringing up the rear. What we saw was scary, to say the least, for a London fog had filled the basement. In unscrewing the tap slightly to let out the water, Noah had inadvertently turned it too far, and it had fallen off. White-hot steam was billowing out, and by himself Noah was unable to reach the spigot, let alone prevent the emptying to dryness of the essential pipe half full of water.

Quite calmly but spitting his words out fast, Noah told each boy where to find gloves to protect their hands, how to hand him the spigot and help him stem the steam and find the thread of the tap so that the spigot could be replaced. Without fuss and in silence they obeyed his instructions and it was over. Noah hugged them both indiscriminately, and he and I turned to include Sam in our arms. The older boys had helped, had worked as a team with him, and Noah was grateful to both. We looked at each other over the three heads, two dark and one blond, and smiled. The moment was balm in my heart.

I have said before how important is the father's sensitivity in our sort of family setup. It is crucial that he be sensitive towards his own son, who possibly has feelings of rejection when he visits what was once his own home, and who needs to adjust to the strange female and new stepbrothers or stepsisters; but the father must also consider his wife, who has her own adjustment problems to handle as well as the task of holding the family together in some way so that the sanity of all is maintained.

Quarrels with a new wife are almost inevitable;

unless, of course a man hides his resentments until they burst forth, at the wrong moment, most likely, snowballed out of all proportion. My own personal view, after growing up in an English society where it was not polite to show one's feelings, anger in particular, is that it is far healthier to express anger at the moment it is felt, than to control it, hold it in, and try to forget its cause. It is unlikely that it will be completely forgotten; rather, it will return to cause trouble later. On the other hand, anger expressed is anger forgotten. And I don't feel it hurts children too much to see this happen, if there is love the rest of the time. Oh, of course, I don't mean completely uncontrolled and frequent anger. But anger is a reality of life, an emotion children themselves experience. Surely it is better for them to do so without guilt, to see that adults have the same feelings and impulses and that it is not very serious to sound off on occasion.

Love and generosity to others must follow the fireworks, however. If anger is the dominant emotion, it is corrosive to all it touches. The husband and father in a stepfamily can do a great deal to make this anger, or resentment, or hurt feelings, or guilt, all seem less important than respect, affection, a good belly laugh, friendship, and love. He can make real to the children the fact that his feelings towards mother and stepmother transcend momentary quarrels.

    We certainly had quarrels—barrels of them. But Noah made up for these in many ways,—by his demonstrated love for me and his nurturing of me as a person, by his awakening me from the shadowy sort of amenable mouse I had been, and his forcing me to use my mind, his encouragement and help in finding free lance research, editing, and writing jobs, and by his basic goodness, generosity, and deepseated affection for my two sons. There were many other more mundane and material things he did for me. Two, in particular, come to mind, and I would like to pass them on.

    The first is important in the context of this book because it had the effect of making me take the trouble to be knowledgeable in an area of interest to small boys—baseball. We lived in Brooklyn, at that time the stronghold of the Dodgers—the famous Bums. Of course Noah and the boys were red-hot fans (even though they felt no interest in fulfilling his dream of having a son in the big leagues). Quite often we subwayed to a game at Ebbets Field, devoured lukewarm hot dogs, were made more thirsty by too sweet soda pop, and scattered peanut shells with the rest of the fans.

    Noah's presents to me were frequently spectacular, among them a fur-lined leather suit and a dress made from a rug. What he gave me on our first anniversary bordered on genius: a share of Giant stock, that is, to be accurate, one share of common and one of preferred in the National Exhibition Company, since it could only be bought in one unit. It was sneaky clever of him. My club was not the Dodgers. This made it possible for the boys and me to indulge in competition and rivalry, but fairly and in friendly fashion, with an objective rather than subjective focus. So Cindy and I joined that maverick breed of Giant fans (I have still not had the heart to sell, although after the club moved to San Francisco my $150 worth of stock mounted to almost $900 before it settled down again). I got so that I knew most of the players on all the teams—it was then a blessedly simple era with only sixteen clubs to keep track of. I enjoyed my new expertise and developed a genuine interest (that most of my girl friends couldn't believe was for real). And in particular I valued the light of respect flickering in the boys' eyes. Noah, of course, got a tremendous belt out of it all.

 The second thing was one of the ways in which Noah showed his feelings to me, that was apparent, in the open, for the boys to see. Perhaps five years after the stock purchase, when he and I were having a rather bumpy time of it, he discovered that for a dollar a week, four dollars a month, he could have a standing order for flowers to be delivered to the house. Before this he had on occasion picked up a bunch of daffodils in spring, of 'mums in fall, to give me on his return from the office. But rarely is there a florist conveniently placed along the route. And rarely does the gesture occur to a tired husband. I found it a marvelous boost to morale to open the door each Saturday morning to a delivery boy holding a bunch of irises one week, roses another, whatever the season was. Weekend hours—harder for a wife than any other family member because everyone is home, to be fed, clothed, and cosseted all at once—can be lightened by this regular demonstration of a husband's thoughtfulness. And it is difficult to stay resentful, self-pitying, irritable, or out of sorts with oneself and the world when arranging flowers so kindly ordered by perhaps the object of the resentment.

X

We were lucky. Andrew's move from the asphalt, soot-covered city school to the verdant Berkshire Mountains boarding school achieved for him all we had hoped, and more. We could brush away the guilty back-of-the-mind whisper that we had taken this step to make it easier for ourselves, that perhaps what he really needed was more familial love and encouragement, not less of it. Transplanting the boy out of the swirl of conflicting emotions loose around him, differing theories of education and upbringing, of address and behavior and manners, could only have been salutary and permitted him to give his very own tastes and aspirations, his drive and talents a free rein. At the school he was guided, of course, by objective though highly interested and intrigued masters, whose classes Andrew pepped up no end.

Even his first year proved a good one, ending with his being awarded *the* prize for first-year students. He excelled in sports as well as in school work, making each season's varsity teams even before his senior year. It was almost magic, the change that had been wrought, as though an imprisoned falcon had been allowed to fly away. And from the first day he set foot in the freshman dormitory to the last, when he was editor of the school paper, senior proctor on a corridor of lower classmen, and valued by master and student alike, he presented no disciplinary problems whatsoever. Even the train episode, which I will describe later, did nothing to dispel the aura of responsibility, involvement, and energy that emanated from him.

Of course our relationship changed, and immeasurably for the better. He came home for an occasional weekend, spent Christmas and Easter vacations with us, and perhaps a week at the end of each long summer. But now there were relatively few days in which it could be said that Andrew was in my charge. Probably just as well. An adolescent is like a prickly pear at best, the sweetness at the core sometimes hard to dig out, though piercing when one succeeds. It was a time when the shape of our feelings was undefined, when we had no need to probe them, when they could lie winter dormant so that, hopefully, a more objective attitude on both our parts could sprout and grow.

It was during this time, when I was free of the daily irritations and conflict that the child Andrew had presented, that I could begin to appraise the past, even appreciate the positive aspects, which really had existed, of our relationship, reassess my role and his, and make plans for our future during his adolescence, even look forward to Andrew the man. I don't mean that abrasiveness, like a nail file at hand in one's pocket, wasn't present beneath the surface, readily produceable on the instant when provoked. It was. But the long absences, during which Andrew had no practice in honing his hostility to me as well as his emotions generally towards his parents, did accomplish a softening, a balance in his outlook on his life and the place in it held by the adults connected with him.

Andrew was happier, far more successful on every level than he had ever been before, interesting other adults as well as his parents, but lacking the intense focusing on himself to which he'd been subjected before. Not that he had minded this, consciously, but it had had the effect of structuring each situation. Andrew was rarely torn apart these days by his own war with authority, and though his need for attention, love, and approval was still present, it was like other people's, more under control.

With Andrew's arrival at Hotchkiss, a new establishment swam into our orbit. Once more I tried to lay in a store of factual information about the school, its mores, tenets, its inmates and surroundings. What resulted was a hodgepodge, like the paraphernalia in a ball player's equipment bag containing not only the bat and mitt of his trade, but the windbreaker, chewing gum or tobacco, bandaids, socks, and T-shirt. I don't think I informed myself consciously, as "a good thing to do," for I was interested intrinsically, especially because Nick might also go there—as he did two years later. But from my past experience, I thought that the boys would appreciate, or at least be helped in some amorphous way by this interest. Then too, it served to impress my husband (whose memory didn't cling to such trivia), who could turn to me at any time to find out who Andrew's English master had been last year, who his roommates were, who was that boy who had been kicked out whom Andrew tried to help, who was captain of the soccer team when Andrew was the center forward, who the huge black dog belonged to, and so on. I was building up credit.

During Andrew's first two years in boarding school, Nick remained at Brooklyn Friends (when he completed eighth grade, he too journeyed up with Andrew in September to the austere halls amid beautiful rolling hills that was Hotchkiss).

Nick missed Andrew, and he missed also the partial anonymity that had been his with the older boy in the house. But it was true that in many ways he benefited during the two years without him, for he was also without the competition, the measuring of himself beside Andrew, and from which we, in spite of the obvious ill-service it did them both, could not refrain. The intensity was not there, the friction, the emotional roller coaster quality of life with Andrew around. Noah was less involved in the children's goings-on. He treated the boys with amused affection, and a friendly but sometimes teasing attitude.

Nick continued to try to please; his uncertainty over what was wanted of him by Noah, and his naturally deliberate way of talking, developed into the rather misleading "playing it cool" appearance that has become a part of him, and that irritated his stepfather, who was accustomed to his own and Andrew's lightning quick thinking and decision-making.

But Noah's partisanship towards conservative externals in the way of educational systems and approaches grew geometrically, with Andrew attending once more a traditionally English sort of school. Noah was always a conservative dresser, and as I have written before, his taste in clothing for boys followed the same pattern. But at the school that Nick attended, Brooklyn Friends, provided you looked neat and clean, no uniform of any kind was required; certainly there was no adherence to the gray flannels and jackets worn by Andrew. Here once more loomed the difference in outlook, attitude, and upbringing. If Noah and I had married at an earlier time, with the three boys all ours, we'd have worked out a mutual way of looking at things long before the time of their adolescence. It is hard to bring two strains together and encourage them to run along smoothly. My tastes in dress were similar to my husband's, though I wouldn't have made much of a point of it had my children wished to dress otherwise. But not only did Nick's school not follow the traditionally held schoolboy fashions, Martin Links, his father, did not either. So of course this meant the boy was torn between what he did and what he actually wanted to do.

   Nick's best friend was Daniel, of the duckbill haircut and flashy clothes. His brilliantined wave fell low on his forehead. None of this Ivy League jazz for him. Both Noah and I liked him, but

Noah tried to counteract the boy's tastes with Nick. There was O'Brien, the prim math whiz, too—whom Noah made fun of. Of course these attitudes met with rebellion from a boy of 13. Then Noah tried to persuade his stepson to say "sir" and "Ma'am," as *he* had done in his Midwest public school, and as Andrew and his friends did automatically at Collegiate or Hotchkiss. It wasn't customary at Friends, however, and Nick did not knuckle under. I too resented this; what rankled, with me, was Noah's not trying to understand the boy (I felt); I was sure that if it had been Andrew, there would have been a greater attempt at empathy.

Several years later, while at Hotchkiss, Nick took a creative writing course. One of his efforts was a story set in this period of his life and in it figured Daniel and his brother Jack, a friend of Andrew's in the past. Jack belonged to a Brooklyn gang, and Daniel was a junior hanger-on. Nick yearned to belong also, to wear the wide, buckled garrison belt, to swear, intimidate, and shoulder smaller kids off the sidewalk. He was held back by the web of inhibitions, cultural clichés and credos, and of course by fear. Clearly his resentment against his home, with its tenets and mores that he was struggling against, and most of all his own weakness and inability to rebel effectively, turned him during this period of his life into a sullen and introverted boy. It was at this time that he made a request that shook me back on my heels; for Nick there was not much emotional pleading—one question, perhaps five minutes of discussion, and that would be that. He would not beg much, or continue trying to persuade. But he did badly want to leave Brooklyn and live on Long Island with his father. I, certainly unwilling to hold him with me against his will, first discussed the matter with his father, and then consulted a child psychiatrist. I talked to her more than once; Martin did once, and Nick met her once. Then Martin and I talked to her together. At the conclusion of these sessions her verdict was that on the whole it would be best for him to stay on with his mother. And that is what we did.

But it wasn't a happy time for Nick. He did react against Noah's strictures, for example, against the crew haircut that Noah liked on him. I remember too, one night that Daniel stayed over. In the morning, Nick lent him one of the despised blue buttondown shirts. A week later Nick was sporting the laundered pink shirt his friend had left behind.

Nick sat his examination for Hotchkiss alone in his eighth grade classroom. (At Collegiate, almost half or more of Andrew's classmates had left to enter prep school at ninth grade.) Nick had received no preparation or training for the type of test given, again unlike Andrew's experience. However, he was accepted, with a scholarship. And that September we had two boys in boarding school, one in ninth grade and one in eleventh.

Once more the competitiveness was there, on Nick's part in particular, because, I have to think, of his need for Noah's approval, respect, and more than anything, his interest. And he did indeed excel at Hotchkiss; both boys during their four years ranged between second and eighth in their class of between 95 and 100 boys, both were varsity athletes in all seasons, both edited the paper, both were responsible, respected leaders in the community. Andrew, the boy of earlier disciplinary problems, helped establish a proctoring system in which older boys had their rooms on the lower class boys' corridor and acted as counselors. He also helped set up a lecture series, held Saturday nights, at which stimulating and famous people in the neighborhood or at the school itself shared their experiences and thoughts with the boys, the masters, and families of the school. Nick was throughout his four years there on the student council. And he won *the* class prize each year he was there.

Noah considered Nick "an eager beaver," as he

called it, and of course he kidded him (and me).
So the boy began to simmer down what I had
found usually a rather attractive eagerness. And
then his stepfather would say: "I wish Nick
wouldn't play it so cool." I minded. I even tried
to point all this out to my husband, to explain to
him that what I believed the boy wanted most was
his stepfather's interest, respect, and involvement.
For many years, however, the two of them were
like male porcupines with each other, their quills
sticking out in all directions and nothing between
them working quite smoothly. At the last, when
Nick had finished college and had in fact "grown
up," there was a dramatic change.

At Hotchkiss the boys might be called friendly
rivals, though the two years between them de-
emphasized their competitiveness. In many ways
they were very close. One weekend when the two
of them had come home, Noah brought to the
house some phonograph record albums. There
were some old-time Wobbly songs, some United
Mineworker songs—in particular *Me Johnny
Mitchell Man*, which became a favorite. But the
album we all enjoyed the most and played
endlessly was entitled *Songs for Sectarians*. In a
gentle and amusing way the songs poked fun at
very serious party adherents of various left-wing
groups; there was "The Cloakworkers Union is

a no-good union . . ." and "The Lady with the Popular Front." But the boys liked best and soon learned by heart the lines of "I knows it, Browder, I knows it, Browder, our line's been changed again." All day long they would sing the refrain to each other; the next day only half of it was used: "Ah knows it, Browder," one boy would say to the other. Next time they were in New York, we heard them address each other as Browd. Although they knew it was the name of the leader of the Communist Party, clearly, to them Browder meant brother; they call each other by this name today, and Nick in particular signs letters with Browd; or Noah asks "How's the Browd?" or to me: "Had a letter from the Browd?"

That the boys could function effectively was being proved to us by their boarding school experience. We had had one occasion already, with the oil burner, in which they handled crisis well. There was another. It was autumn, during an early cold snap, when Noah suffered a serious turn of fortune. It occurred to a dedicated master of boys at Hotchkiss that it would help Nick and Andrew, and their parents, if they could spend the weekend together at this time.

Saturday after class the three of them drove down to the city. We made the most of the unexpected visit. And Sunday evening, after an early supper, the boys were picked up for the ride back to school. Noah and I blessed Mr. Ramsey for his understanding of the worries of boys and parents, and sat staring into the cannel coal fire. We were on the way to bed, around eleven o'clock, when the telephone rang.

"I know it's terribly late, Mr. Joplin, but I didn't want you to worry. I was afraid you might have telephoned the boys and found them still out. Everything's okay now, and there's nothing to worry about."

Of course, hearing my husband's puzzled and laconic responses, I had visions of a hospital operating room at the very least. We learned then only that Mr. Ramsey had struck a drunk on the road and knocked him unconscious; that he had, helped by Nick and Andrew, taken the man to a hospital, and only arrived back at the school after eleven. Later the master told us how he had begun to shake, after hitting the man, whose life may well have been saved by the amount of liquor in him. Mr. Ramsey told us that the boys had helped him knit up his shattered nerves, and in an impressively mature way had handled themselves and given him encouragement so that they had all been able to proceed. We were proud of them.

Andrew, by this time, no longer went to camp

during the summer months. For two summers he had worked as a caddy in a posh Hollywood golf course, earning over $1,000 each time, while living with his mother in Los Angeles. At 16 he signed on as seaman on an oil tanker. Our Clarence Day father believed in early exposure to life's harsh realities. Nick did say to me once that sometimes he wished he was able to spend all summer at the beach, sailing, swimming, partying, as most of the other boys in his class seemed to enjoy. Actually, though, I doubt that they really regret those summers of work—for Nick went to sea also.

Andrew's characteristic reaction to the sledgehammer "Dear John" letter from his first love—a useful and commendable one that was to be followed in the future and stand him in good stead—was to bury himself in his work. His grades shot up. His involvement in the life of the school became even greater, and it was then that he thought through the idea of the proctor system and broached the school faculty on bringing speakers such as nature writer Hal Borland, cartoonist Robert Osborne, author Stephen Birmingham, to lecture to the school community.

I have said that Andrew and Nick had very different attitudes towards the absent members of their family. This was pointed up sharply in the way each boy dealt with writing home. Nick wrote to both families separately and infrequently, letters that rarely if ever mentioned one of the Long Island contingent to me, for example, or vice versa. Andrew, on the other hand, would make a carbon and send original to one parent, copy to the other. (He does it to this day, and I still mind.) In addition, he freely acknowledged both to each other, saying "tell Mom this . . ." or "ask Mom when she's coming up." It was *my* name that he'd rarely use.

Nevertheless, although Andrew tried desperately to think of his parents as united and to act as though they were, his whole Hotchkiss experience was a part of his life with us, his father and stepmother, rather than with both his natural parents. This was tacitly recognized by us all, though there was nothing calculated on anyone's part in it being so. We were the ones who went on the journey with him for his initial interview, who took him there when he entered as a new boy, who knew the boys' and masters' names and what they taught, who came to watch the soccer game when Andrew's headed goal won for the school, the track meets, the French plays. I read the *Record* (the school paper) assiduously, and passed on its tidbits to Noah, and in other ways put my homework to good use.

But it is possible that a stepchild might resent

his stepmother's putting her finger into all his pies, and Andrew quite possibly did—far more, in any case, than if I were his real mother. Again, while being sensitive to what might legitimately cause hostility, and acting accordingly, it is the wise stepmother who will try to stick to a course of conduct and an attitude towards her stepson that she feels is the right one for her. Above all, she must not dither. I probably in some ways was less secure with my natural sons than I was with Andrew. In my relationship with him, my problem was sticking to my guns, and avoiding asking myself all the time whether I was right or wrong, mean, not understanding, and so on, and therefore being and acting utterly inhibited and unlike myself.

I think a young person hates uncertainty and shillyshallying on the part of a grown-up more than anything else. Give him someone he can dislike, whose rules he can rebel against, any day, rather than one who gives an order and then is wheedled out of it, who sets the rules and then allows the stepchild to change his or her mind.

Andrew's mother Cora had perhaps journeyed up five or six times during his four years at the school. She did of course go to his graduation, with us, as did a girl for the dance. But although he did his best, as Noah did, to make it a good time for her, it must have been hard and lonely, as well as embarrassing. For me it was awkward; I can remember today the feeling of being a person apart when she, Andrew, and Noah went off together and talked for a while. How much more so must she have felt this way. I would have stayed out of the picture to the point of not going, so that the boy could have had his parents completely to himself—but Noah would not hear of this. I disagreed, but complied with his wish to include me in. Yet—fools that we mortals be, when the three of them did go off, at the dance, and sit and chat together, I felt left out and embarrassed in my turn.

Nick's father Martin did come up to Hotchkiss for Father's days and also on occasion to watch his son at soccer or track. But again, it was more our world than his. He approached Nick's masters as a father, typically inquiring about his son's progress. At the time of Nick's arrival, two years into the six we spent driving between New York and Lakeville, Connecticut, we were on first-name basis with several of the masters, and we also had a professional connection with one or two, helping them market books. And, in addition, we loved the surrounding countryside and wished to be part of it even when our sons departed therefrom. So we bought an old red farmhouse across the state line in Massachusetts, a little further into the benign folds of the Berkshire Mountains.

I have already described the ways in which the boys were competitive; perhaps it would be more accurate to say that Nick, being the younger, willy-nilly gave the appearance of striving to catch up with his stepbrother. They did indeed compete in one way or another, and match up throughout their years at the school. Each achievement was accomplished with, in Andrew's case, an eye backward over his shoulder to make sure Nick wasn't overtaking him, and in Nick's, the redoubled effort to draw alongside. Their accomplishments were spectacular. Yet I never felt they were in any sense rivals, in spite of their involvement in each other. If anything, they gave each other strength, comradeship, and support when needed. I believe each would have withdrawn in the other's favor had the two of them alone competed for one particular prize. I have often wondered what would happen if they both fell for the same girl. There was one time that Andrew got into trouble at Hotchkiss—the only time (I cannot even remember a censure for untidiness, which can hardly be said of Nick), and Nick was at his side.

The school enforced vigorously its rules against smoking and drinking, not only on the premises, but on school trains bearing boys to and fro as well. It was at the end of the Christmas vacation—that desperate time of year when the gloomy desolation of winter gives no whisper yet of approaching spring—and the boys were returning to Lakeville by train. Schoolboys, like adults, are affected by the barren drabness around them. The merriment of Christmas, over and done with along with the discarded Christmas trees, added to everyone's sense of depression. When cans of beer were passed up and down the aisle of the train, Andrew and Nick shared one with the rest. Unfortunately not everyone was quiet about it, and some disgruntled adult whose destination was reached before Lakeville telephoned the authorities when he got off and reported the raucous carryings-on. When the train pulled into the school station, the Assistant Head Master was there, grim-faced. That Nick, member of the Student Council, was aboard, together with Andrew, also a member and chairman of the paper, didn't cheer him up. Names were taken. Next day Nick resigned his post, Andrew following him. It was a month at least before both boys were reinstated.

The applications for college followed the pattern of those for prep school, with blank spaces for father; mother; stepfather; stepmother.

In the request for autobiographical material, both Andrew and Nick took them literally. They wrote about their parents' divorce and their subsequent mixed-up existence. Andrew did not voice to me any resentments against his parents. I know he felt some towards Noah on occasion, but he never voiced them about Cora, nor would I have asked him. His written comment was a straightforward though introspective and analytic account, and he was aided in its details by his father.

Nick's application form also arrived at home while he was there. And he too planned to include the part his parents' divorce played in his life. "Why did you get a divorce?" he asked.

This was a Brazil nut to crack. His father had not beaten me, nor deceived me, nor had I him. How can one pinpoint reasons for the vortex of the atmosphere between two people that becomes stormy to the point of one or both of them wanting a divorce? And how, in particular, to describe its reasons to the issue of that broken union? It was almost impossible to be completely honest about it, to arrive at the real core of the reason or reasons, to give him an answer that was truthful and meaningful and yet one which would not hurt. Parents might well take the time to work this out for themselves, because it is likely they will be posed the question sooner or later, if they are on reasonably good terms with their offspring, and it usually comes out of the blue, too.

I will disclose one thing I told Nick, because I feel it might be useful to others. It was of course only part of the answer. I told him that his father had been unable to show anger at me when he felt it, usually for perfectly justifiable reasons. Instead, he bottled it all up, so that it built up a pressure of resentment against me. This had happened to the point of poisoning the atmosphere, and we just were not getting on. It was not that Martin was characteristically a particularly mild sort of person. But he had grown up believing that outbursts of anger and irritation should be controlled, that they were childish. And so he had never been able to bat me down when I needed it.

I told this to Nick, because he is woven out of the same cloth. My belief, already expressed, is that rigid control of anger is self-destructive, and I passed this theory on to my son. Nick therefore wrote of his parents' divorce in those terms.

Andrew, during his last year at Hotchkiss, having already been accepted at Harvard, was taking an advanced "creative writing" course. He was given special permission in the course to present part of a novel as his term's work. I do not recall very much of Andrew's effort, which he made a point of showing me! All I do remember is the description of an unsympathetic character named Marianne who lay on a couch all day long, nursing her arthritic limbs and reading *The New York Times*. It gave me the feeling—when Andrew had handed the manuscript to me to read—that I was prying into someone's correspondence, with a sign ". . . readers see no good of themselves" printed in block letters slipped in between the pages.

Nevertheless, this period brought rewards for me. Andrew turned to me for counsel, for my appraisal on what happened, what was said, what was meant. I think he was beginning to value my restraint, my way of looking at a girl's point of view as well as his, my feminine intuition perhaps. And he was developing some objectivity as regards his parents. When their ideas differed from his own, he was beginning to be able to assess the situation and make a choice for himself. Without worrying about disloyalty. For one thing, his mother wasn't around, and besides, her attitudes differed from mine on many matters. I think with one's own children one tends to want their desires fulfilled, and it is hard to be objective. So it is at this period in a young person's life that the step-relationship can pay off—if over the years the hostility and resentment have been held within reasonable bounds.

At some point it is likely that an adolescent will take a new look at his stepmother and grow to realize her possible value to him, if their relationship has been conducted fairly, in spite of initial differences and lack of mutual understanding. If the stepmother has held on to her own identity through thick and thin, despite her husband's wishes, her stepchild's whim, or her desire to keep the peace—now is the time that a rich harvest may be there for the picking.

Suddenly a growing boy will find his eyes seeing different things, and will possibly take the hand held out in friendship and counsel, a hand that once he believed only wanted to chastise or admonish him. And so I must repeat my dictum to stepmothers: hold on fast to your own nature; if you are retiring and nonaggressive, stay that way. These traits will be appreciated later on. You will suddenly seem to be a marvelously sturdy rock to cling to; perhaps a vessel of serenity, or a Solomon. I had tried not to be emotional with Andrew; he had been aware of my frequent disapproval or discomfort, and now he was beginning to feel respect for my sense of values. He no longer distrusted my motives. And when I voiced an opinion, he began to take it seriously. And this is what it is all about, somehow. I felt rewarded.

One's mother, one likes or dislikes—but as a rule one accepts her. One doesn't have to accept a stepmother. As time goes by, she can be ignored, even. But when her opinions are sought after, they have an importance that she must realize, and she must therefore take care not to give them carelessly.

XI

If I had to pick one cardinal rule to be followed by all stepparents, whether father or mother, it would be this: *Never, never, never criticize or diminish to your child in any way the absent, now divorced other parent.* It can achieve nothing good and might do immeasurable harm to a boy or girl desperately missing his absent mother or father and hopelessly confused about the rights or wrongs of it all. Because this parent is not with him, he will probably idealize him. *Both* his parents are the most important people that he knows.

Children, as they mature, begin to see their parents as human beings instead of the gods in their life, with the same grandeur as before, perhaps, but now with the same failings as everyone else. It is usually a difficult aspect of growing up, to look one day at these wonderful and important creatures and see that they actually have clay feet. But the change of attitude is crucial. Growing up is a slow process, as a rule, but all of us must go through it, and on our own. No one else can do it for us.

The unhappy months of separation that culminate in divorce, during which his mother is learning how to operate on two wheels instead of four, is a traumatic experience for her child. But if it doesn't destroy him—and children are blessedly hardy little animals who accept what life dishes out for them on the whole, and adapt to it successfully—this difficult time will give him a big push up that ladder he must climb to maturity. To confront him with adult bitterness, hatred, accusations about experiences and situations he cannot or should not know anything about, and understands less, is, I believe, highly destructive and therefore thoroughly selfish on the part of the adult who gives way to them in front of him.

What I am saying about natural parents criticizing their ex-spouses also, of course, applies to a new wife or husband criticizing the natural parent of her or his stepchild—it can only have a ruinous effect on future relations if you, his stepmother, whom he is learning to live with, to like, love, and respect, voices or implies criticism of his blood mother.

The man and woman able to go through separation, divorce, and possibly remarriage without feeling deep-seated bitterness and rancor are relatively few and far between. They are the lucky ones, who can wrap themselves in a cloak of dignity and pride, and concentrate on making that dead air period following divorce as easy as possible for the children involved. To adults, everything may seem to roll along, at least on the surface, on greased wheels. But it is very different and hard to understand for a child whose mother and father no longer live in the same house, who now at best talk politely to each other when they meet, as though they were strangers. He must feel like a shuttlecock being batted to and fro between them.

    I believe strongly that it is important for parents to develop with full awareness a conscious attitude towards their divorced mates, an attitude of considerateness and "gentlemanliness." This will help the child's love and respect for both parents to flower, without guilt. For children frequently blame themselves for their parents' divorce.

    Practical questions needing discussion are going to come up daily. You may divorce a man, but unless you are willing to do irreparable damage to your child by pretending his father no longer exists, you cannot really avoid seeing him, talking to him, writing to him, and thinking of him fairly constantly as your children and his grow up. It will be painful, irritating, a bore, a cause for moodiness, or rift with the present spouse, but it all has to be gone through. It is a price to be paid, and far less of one than what the child, willy-nilly, has been forced into.

It is not unusual for a mother to believe quite honestly that her ex-husband is bad for her children, that her duty lies in trying to help them forget that they are related equally to another person, whom they do not see or communicate with "because it is best for them." However, I think all the professionals in the field of child psychiatry, guidance, and counseling agree this "divorce" from his father rarely is "best" for the child. If the child is brought up reasonably well, at the time he has grown up, or before—whenever he has gained enough experience and wisdom to evaluate people, to balance one against the other, to compare their performances, to understand his own needs and how those in his family meet or do not meet these needs—he will make this decision for himself, will himself decide whom he wants to see and whom not. It is an arduous task for a parent bringing up a child with the other parent missing much of the time, but perhaps the supreme one, to keep open for him this freedom of choice.

Yet the withholding of a child from his natural father is practiced all around us with horrible frequency. Let me say here that I am not in support of present husband-penalizing alimony laws, and do agree with Charles Metz, author of *Divorce and Custody for Men* (Doubleday, 1968), that fathers often are as capable or more capable than mothers of caring for the children, and that custody awards to mothers should not be nearly as automatic as they are today.

Unless there is absolutely no contact or communication between the divorced parents of a child, whether because of death, distance, or one parent's forcing separation between the *child* and non-custodial parent, certain matters must be considered and discussed by both, even if not agreed upon, in their mutual concern and interest over their offspring: these matters include *visitation*; *money*; *education*; *religion*; *illness*.

The rules under which an absent parent may see his children are usually laid down in the separation agreement and divorce settlement with his ex-partner. How this is handled, how these rules are followed, whether to the letter or the spirit, and how pleasantly, depends on the extent of the goodwill between the parents. Visits take place for the day, for the weekend, over Christmas or Easter vacation, or extended periods such as one or three months during the summer time. The meeting of ex-mates is often unavoidable, and if it is avoided, this in itself is awkward and noticeable to the child. It is embarrassing at the best of times. If one or both partners determine to make it as difficult as possible, it will most likely poison at least part of the precious time allotted child and visiting or visited parent. The point to remember as being of paramount importance is the welfare of the child. His welfare is certainly not being considered if he is the unwilling listener to acrimony, no matter how fleeting. Nor is it helpful if he is forced to explain to his visiting father what are clearly fabricated roadblocks set up by his mother, or unreasonable attitudes towards his father's plans for day or weekend.

Unhappily, the bitterness of divorce and all its implications makes some of us myopic and self-deluding. I myself know of at least three examples of children who never even saw their father after the divorce of the parents. In two of the cases, the mother made it part of the separation agreement. In the other, the father never came around, literally divorcing his child as well as his wife. In this case the mother, sensing the child's at first articulated and then unspoken hurt, bought presents and birthday cards and pretended Dad had sent them. As the child grew older, this pretence became too obvious to keep up. Finally, after this mother remarried, the boy was only too happy to belong to a father, even if not the real one, and he took his stepfather's name. One doesn't have to be endowed with extraordinary imagination to realize what this boy had gone through, what doubts, confusion, identity crises, and trauma. Fortunately his mother is a stable and serene woman, as well as a loving one, and whatever could be done to make up for this unerasable knowledge she does, with the help of an affectionate and intelligent stepfather and a whole brood of half-sisters.

I have another friend, who went on one of his regular visits to see his son, only to find that the boy and his mother had vanished. After years of anguished searching and costly fees to detectives, he discovered their whereabouts. But the sorrow had blunted, and he felt it wise to wait until the child was more mature before disrupting his life any further. He played it smart, this father. Learning that his son's maternal grandmother had died, he sent flowers and signed his name—the same as his son's. The boy, now 16, questioned his mother, who had over the years left him with the idea his father was dead. She had no answer for him. The other day my friend described to me the visit of his son for the weekend, and how the tears streamed down his face when he saw the boy walk towards him from the plane. And now his son wishes to come and live with his father; the mother, who rationally cannot refuse, is making this possible.

Then there is my Chicago friend Brian Folsom, who sat out an unhappy marriage for a long time until he fell in love and wanted out. The apparently unending hatred on the part of his first wife—in spite of the fact that she remarried as soon as he did, to a man with money, yet still demanded her dollars, cents, and ounces of flesh and put every difficulty in the way of visitation—seems very hard to believe or understand.

Because of visitation difficulties made because she seriously believed Brian was bad for their three children, the matter had to go to court, and not just once. This meant, too, that the children had to be in court. They have been interviewed and questioned by court-appointed psychiatrists. They have had periods—now happily over—of being so confused, they were unwilling even to talk with their natural father on the telephone, let alone see him when he entered their mother's house to fetch the youngest. They were instructed, and disobedience was not possible at the age all this began, to call Patrick, their stepfather, Dad, even though when they visited with their natural father Brian they obviously called him Dad also.

When the boys reached Little League age, Brian went to watch, and was embarrassed, not to say horrified, to get the point from their mother and stepfather that no gesture, even a wave or a smile, was to be sent his way, though he was sitting with the two children of his second marriage, indisputably half-brothers of those living with the mother.

Brian was puzzled, and very unhappy as he attempted to plough through a rocky weekend bull-session with his children, who were explaining why they really shouldn't visit him and Mary very often. After all, they said, except for him, whom they could see in the city perhaps, they were not related at all.

"What about Joe and baby Sandy?" their father asked.

"Joe and Sandy are no relatives of ours. Dad—I mean *Patrick*, said so."

Gulping a bit, Brian explained at some length and with considerable emphasis that on the contrary Joe and Sandy were very much half-brothers of theirs, and they'd better believe it. Their father was *their* father. They had no other *real* father, nor did Joe and Sandy. Ergo—they were related. Brian shook his head in frustration once again at the continuing grievance nursed against him by his children's mother.

Some children take pleasure in passing on

information calculated to upset the listener and make him angry at his ex-mate. Clearly such children, who are usually started on this unsavory path by injudicious or mischievous questioning, have been considerably disturbed by what has happened between their parents. Many more, I would venture, prefer that their parents' meetings be matter-of-fact and uneventful, even if they cannot be pleasant, even if being with Mom and Dad together isn't as comfortable as it used to be.

I have described my stepson Andrew's reaction to the weekly dislocation and whirlpool of emotions that buffeted him in everything implied by the subway ride between Brooklyn and Manhattan. My mind boggles at how he would have withstood it all, if he had had to listen to acrimony and accusations by his father against his mother, or vice versa.

We were fortunate that all five parents in our triple-barreled family situation meant well by the children and were usually pretty successful in implementing this by self-control, considerateness, honesty, and good humor.

It can even happen that amity exists between ex-husbands and wives and their new mates. I was amused by my friend Jane's description. The four grown-ups in her situation get on well, and so do the children, who run in and out of the two New

York City apartments at will. So often do they all see each other, that the younger children are sometimes confused as to who belongs to whom. Jane not only received a Mother's Day card from her own little girl and her two stepchildren, she also had one from the child of her husband's ex-wife and *her* new husband, not related to Jane in *any* way. This makes me realize a minor disadvantage of having only sons (a boon to my way of thinking—the stepmother-stepson relationship is so much easier than that of stepmother and stepdaughter): not until the boys were almost grown up did I, *once*, receive a Mother's Day card. And as for birthdays—well, it was I who would always remind each one of their various parents' birthdays. Facing my own was a dilemma. It is the woman of the house who keeps abreast of such matters. Should I remind them myself? Tell Noah to? Or say nothing and feel neglected?

As I have described, Andrew came to his father every weekend, in the early days. Nick and Sam went out to their father every other weekend, and also spent at least a month in summer with him. As their father and stepmother's family grew, there developed the habit of alternating holidays such as Christmas and Easter. When my boys were more or less grown, we let them spend *every*

Christmas at their father's with the smaller children, since it is a holiday particularly joyous for the young. Andrew was usually with us part of every holiday. The fact that his mother was alone was taken into consideration, so that she could share too some time of celebration with her son.

As the boys matured, they themselves had choices, respected whenever possible. It worked moderately smoothly. But it was always a strain and this sort of dovetailing was never very easy to handle and needed rather careful planning and flexibility when things worked out rather differently. As I tried to emphasize in earlier chapters, this sort of forethought, or preventative planning, is the lot of the wife as a rule. It is all up to her whether it works or not. She'll fret and worry over it, and if she doesn't do it well and smoothly, she'll suffer and be hurt. Take your choice.

Since the three boys' fathers worked in the city, a conference or visit with Dad over lunch was always available to them, and little interference, or none that I can remember, was ever placed in the way of this. So we did not go through any of the agony and constant bickering of the Folsom family over the years.

We didn't have it quite so easy, when it came to money matters. Here too, it is the lawyers who call the tune, and the man and wife, now separated and divorced, must abide by whatever melody they piped, to a greater or lesser degree. It is my belief that money is the greatest impediment there is to decent, well-mannered relationship between ex-partners. It can, and usually does embitter in one way or another both he who gives, whether willingly or by force or law, and she who takes, whether she feels it sufficient or is bitter because she must skimp to get by. And not only does it so affect the two principals, but their current spouses, if such exist. Unless all concerned have plenty of money, it may and probably will influence the climate between divorced parents throughout the growing-up period of their offspring. It touches decisions about education, housing, clothing, vacations, the medical and dental services chosen, and a whole raft of other problems sticky enough in their own right.

Horrible as it may be, money can influence something as important and basic as the decision to have a child. My Seattle friends Nigel and Jennifer Hornsby are in this particular bind. They have three children between them, she one by a previous marriage, he two. They have none together. Jennifer has wanted nothing so desperately as to have a child with her new husband, and not only because she loves him. She wanted her husband's attention centered in *her* home, on *her* children, instead of in the apartment of his ex-wife because that is where his children live. Because of the impossible burden alimony imposes on them, not only could the Hornsbys not afford a child, but during the early years of their marriage Jen was forced to work so they could make ends meet.

Noah and I, while not able to dismiss all thought and worry over money, could not be said to be any way in need. Money certainly did not affect my husband's relationship with his ex-wife, Andrew's mother. This was because *she* would not let it. Cora was utterly ungrasping. Because she worked, she accepted support for Andrew only when he lived with her. After he joined us in Brooklyn, and later went to boarding school, a reasonable lump sum in settlement was worked out. Noah, of course, paid all his son's expenses for school, college, medical costs, and everything else, although like the other boys after him, Andrew began at 14 to work during the summer months and from then on earned his own pocket money— or the major share of it.

I was very fortunate. New wives, as well as old, feel resentment over the precious painstakingly earned money which their husbands must by law send out as support and alimony—a forfeit to the past.

In my own case it was somewhat different. Nick and Sam, whose father and growing family was pinched by a fixed salary, received modest support until they were through college. Because, at the time of my divorce, their father did not believe in private school education, and in any case could not afford it, he did not contribute towards the rather costly education of the two boys. When, since he was not strong, we were advised that private school was in order if at all possible for Sam, his father did make a contribution, though a token one, and did help with medical bills.

Comparatively easy as this prickly matter of money was for us, Noah and I were nevertheless not free from problems caused by it, nor without resentments with money at their core. At one time or another I venture any man, no matter how loving, will resent the presence of another's children, somehow masquerading as his own. And no matter how generous he is, he will resent having to think about their cost in money terms. Unknown to himself, Noah did resent this and let me know it. Not that he begrudged a penny spent on his two stepsons. It wasn't the money itself that caused his resentment, he believed, but the fact that their father was not the one paying it. But however one views it, it *is* the money which is the focus, the core, of the resentment. Similarly, the boys' father must have resented another man's being able to do more for his sons than he could. Because I minded so much being in the middle of these two what seemed to me valid and natural viewpoints, and because in most ways everything else had worked out fairly amicably, I tried in a sense to appease them both. I tried to explain Martin's position to Noah. And, when it was possible, I earned money for the private schools by a piece of research or a rewrite job. If that was not available, I asked my father for what was needed. And so we succeeded over the years in maintaining a friendly enough atmosphere whenever my ex-husband and I saw each other or needed to communicate by phone or letter.

I do remember one occasion when the money situation was causing pretty strained relations, and when Noah was making me feel I was not thinking first of his interests. And so he suggested we meet with Martin, to discuss the whole matter. I couldn't refuse. I can't remember what specifically it was all about. But I do know that the witnessing of and the listening to an ex-husband and a current one engaged in argument over support of one's children by the former require more intestinal fortitude than I possess. Never again!

There was one unbudgeable Gibraltar in the soil of our meadow, however. Martin took both boys as tax deductions. He did this automatically from the very beginning. I don't think it occurred to him that there might be any question about this, or to us either. Certainly, in the early years we didn't give it much thought. As the cost of living went up, however, and the boys' expenses rocketed, Noah began to grumble. The time that this sticky point came up was always, of course, in those painful, mathematics-filled and frenetic weeks of record searching before April 15.

"Why didn't *you* take the boys as deductions?" our accountant asked Noah, and he passed on the question to me. It was around the time the law had changed, to state specifically that the deduction is allowable to whichever parent, step or natural, contributes the greatest amount. Objectively, this pointed to us, and I took it up with Martin over the telephone. But to him, the figures had added up differently. So I held my peace. I was unable to be hardboiled about this, unfair though my position was to Noah. It seemed to me that to tell a man he couldn't take his own two sons as tax deductions—when he contributed to their support and never, to his eternal credit, defaulted or was overly late in sending each month—served to deball him. And I didn't want to do it. Noah grumbled, Noah complained, Noah fumed. I fretted, I squirmed, I felt guilty, I cried. But I held to my position, and Noah abided by it; and every spring the accountants nursed their frustrations to no avail. I knew it was utterly inconsistent, this generosity to my former husband at the expense of the present one, whom I loved, but I couldn't help it.

Today I believe this matter is one that should be covered in separation and divorce agreements. As children of divorce mature and time erases much of the old bitterness, most of the petty aggravations between parents diminish in size and decline in number. But the subject of tax deduction is a hardy perennial that will poke its head up like the snowdrop, regularly every March, until the children are out of college or self-supporting.

Unless the terms are very carefully spelled out in the settlement and divorce agreements, it is the parent with custody who makes the ultimate decision on all policy matters. But one parent is wise not to exclude the other, when something important arises to do with their common offspring. It is cruel, pointless and stupid to pretend that the other parent does not exist. It should be possible for parents to get together about these important matters and give each other a chance to air views and argue for their own if necessary. If they are not in the same location, they can telephone, or write. Also, I believe it incumbent on the current spouse to swallow any jealousy or irritation when these meetings take place, *and* keep his or her mouth shut about them.

How the custodial parent educates her children will depend on her philosophy and financial ability. Unless this has been previously specified, it is usually up to the mother, with whom most children of divorce live. If she has strong convictions, whether in support of private schools or public, she will probably be able to act accordingly.

Noah and Cora had no philosophical conflict about schools that I ever heard. They quite simply wanted the best they could find for their clearly gifted son—independent New York City school, prep school, and university. Money was not to stand in their way.

And for my part, I found that many private schools and colleges, at least the well-endowed boys' prep schools, would give scholarships to promising children of parents in the marital and financial situation we were in. After one year of public school, in which Nick did very well, I found I disliked his being one of the teacher's favored few. He had top marks, yes, but never a challenge to his mind, a stretching of his intellectual muscle. So I too began to feel it important that he receive the best possible education. I was helped to do so by very generous aid policies of prep school and university (today, with the nationwide drive to enroll the "culturally deprived," parents in my position are certainly less fortunate and rightly so). Martin did not hold with my wishes for the boys' schooling on principle, although I cannot help but believe his main reason to be financial, since now that his second family is of high school age his outlook has undergone something of a change. But apart from not sharing costs, he put no obstacle in my way and took the appropriate amount of interest in everything they did, wherever it was.

The matter of religion, of church going, of Sunday school, can also be subject for conflict between divorced parents, depending on their beliefs and personal fervor. If the one-time partners were both devout practitioners of their religion, be it Catholic, Protestant, Jewish, or whatever, they know even though one is separated and free from influence or coercion of the previous partner, the pattern will prevail. If they were not, then once more it will be left up to the custodial parent to make the decisions. If he or she remarries and the new spouse imposes his beliefs and practices on his children, of course, the absent father has every right to take this up with the mother. Whether he will have any influence is another story.

Believing it important for children to have some sort of religio-ethical training, Noah and I wished the boys to attend Sunday school. We weren't particular about the denomination. Our own religious backgrounds were almost as mixed as the ethnic makeup of our country—Christian Scientist, Anglican, and Jewish (and both my sisters and their families are Catholic). Both Nick and Sam had attended Riverside Church nursery school, and when we moved to Brooklyn, Sam was entered at the Grace Church (Episcopal) nursery school. For a time Andrew, and Nick after him, went to the Unitarian church on the next block, for long enough at least to earn a black leather-covered Bible with their name tooled in gold on it. And Nick did sing in the Grace Church choir (I still have the little tan-colored paper envelope with a penciled notation by Miss McKittrick, the acerbic choir mistress, attesting to his attendance and the amount of money he earned thereby).

Sam, because he had the years of nursery school there, and many years of Miss Hepburn's dancing class, was completely at home at Grace Church, and familiar with all its personnel. There he was baptized and confirmed. He too was a choir boy. But I never consulted his father about this, in spite of my theoretic opinions expressed above. I was wrong. I presume, now, however, that if Martin had had strong views on the matter, we'd at least have talked about it. But then I neglected even to ask. His second wife was, I believe, Protestant, and with the mixed ethnic and religious heritage, he and his new family attended the Unitarian church where they lived. He, his wife, and three children by that wife, lived in one place, and so attended church in that place. What really made it hard for *us* to stick to any sort of regular church or Sunday school attendance for the three boys was that our weekend pattern differed from week to week. It seemed heartless to insist on Andrew's going alone each Sunday. Besides, he or his mother might well have resented my forcing Episcopalianism on him. The lack of continuity, the differing beliefs and practices, made church going too hard to impose. In Sam's case, he himself wanted to go. I might myself have attended Grace Church with him on a regular basis—we did sometimes go as a family, at Easter and Christmas—but Sunday breakfast was a big deal, and I was too tired, or apprehensive of being too tired, if I went to church first. Gradually we came to a complete *laissez-faire* attitude, and after Nick left the choir the two older boys attended only when we all were going and insisted on their accompanying us.

It is a grievous thing for a man to give up his children. No matter how deep-seated the bitterness surrounding his divorce, no matter who had instigated proceedings, who had originally been at fault, it can only help her children if a mother realizes how very difficult and painful this sudden loss of the fruit of his loins is to a man. If she is able to see this, she will do her best to share the important moments of her children's lives with their natural father. By the same token, she will encourage her second husband to share these moments with *his* first wife, mother of her stepchildren, and not put roadblocks, real or emotional, in his way.

One of these times, traumatic in itself for the suffering child, is when he is ill. I don't of course refer to a common cold, the flu, or a sprained ankle—or even the chicken pox. But any time the child's normal life is disturbed by more serious illness, such as measles, mumps, broken limbs, or anything involving hospitalization, surgery, and its accompanying fear and shock, he deserves if at all possible and practical the emotional backing and support his real parents can give him—both of them.

My stepson Andrew was particularly sweet and

vulnerable when he didn't feel well, and he appreciated the attention I gave him at those times. Noah was happy, and I too, that his frequently open hostility seemed to disappear at these times. I, too, was probably not so edgy, so ready to look for slights, and of course I was aware, as Noah was, of what the child missed, with his natural mother elsewhere. Though not a "born" nurse, as some women are (I knew this, having spent some time as a student nurse in France), I must admit that I enjoy the ministering to people when they are not well. It didn't happen often with Andrew while he was under my roof, for he was a healthy child.

When Nick had his tonsils and adenoids removed, he certainly needed someone during the night—to give him security. Yet I did not think about asking his father to be with him. Clearly, I did not always practice what I now preach.

In those days I stressed my philosophy, bolstered in my belief by Andrew's asking for the opposite, that the reality situation is what should be put before the child, so that no dream of his parents' reuniting can take root. But in times of illness, I feel this can and should temporarily be put to one side. Most of us believe by now that mental and emotional well-being has an effect on the physical condition. Children are so vulnerable when they are not well.

I have described above where I think parents, no matter how, when, or why separated, should get together, for their children's weal, on matters of policy, attitudes, philosophy. There are other times, situations really, when they are also likely to meet, or should meet or communicate in some fashion in their children's interest. These can be at PTA meetings at the schools their children attend, on prize days, Parents' Day, athletic events, and graduations. These occasions may be embarrassing or awkward for adults and perhaps their children too. It would be well for them to take the time to think about their child, his character, personality, emotional fortitude, and weaknesses, even his attitude towards them and their divorce, before deciding on just what course they intend to follow. They may, depending on circumstance and their child's psychological attitude, attend affairs together; or they can take turns showing up at his prize day or when the Nativity play is put on by his class. In later years it can be a help to consult the child as to his wishes.

Our three boys reacted very differently. Andrew wanted his own two parents together. As I've already described, he liked to think to himself that they were still together—as he obviously so held them in his heart. He'd accept my attendance at functions if need be, for want of anyone "better" belonging to him.

Nick did not want at all to be confronted with two sets of parents at the same time, though we didn't realize this for a number of years. His father and I usually took turns at school functions, though I can remember occasions at Friends School when Nick was performing in plays and his father and I sat at different spots in the auditorium and bowed politely to each other when our eyes met. This need for separateness in his worlds persisted through college.

Sam, who had by far the most "normal" growing up, for a child of divorce that is, does not look back to any resentment or bitterness about what had happened to his parents, to any sense of deprivation or resentment. This is why, frankly, there is less about him in this book. Apart from transitory discomfort, because he was no longer the baby in his father's house and he took quite a few years to appreciate the children of that home, Sam enjoyed all the grown-ups of his world. (Recently he told me of his great pleasure now when he receives letters from his half-sister and half-brother.) He felt little resentment at his stepfather Noah or his stepmother Ann, and so it was satisfying, even jolly for him when they both attended his various school functions, dropped in at dancing school, sat in together on Parents' Day. All of us went to his graduation from prep school. Here, unlike his brother Nick, who hated being the center of adoring eyes, he enjoyed having us surround him and thump him on the back in proud congratulation. It was his half-sister Jane, at 13, who found the situation awkward and was self-conscious about it, not Sam.

Andrew's graduation from Hotchkiss, while awkward for me and his mother, perhaps even distressing for her since she was unaccompanied, was a happy time, really. Andrew was pleased as punch with us all, at the pride and admiration of his three attendant parents and his girl friend— invited for the senior dance. It was the same when he received his university diploma with a magna attached.

Nick disliked the intensity of parental pride focused on him at such occasions. He did not know, however, just how to avoid it during the celebrations ending his secondary school life. And so he endured it all somehow, though as I remember unusually gracelessly, for him, with Noah and I, and girl friend (it didn't help matters that he was on the outs during the whole two days with her, too—or perhaps he wanted it that way to make his misery complete?) and father and stepmother attending ceremonies and prize giving. But the memory of his suffering was not expunged by four years of higher learning, and so he left the university before graduation ceremonies, preferring to have his diploma mailed to him. Had I been more aware, more acute and considerate, or less self-conscious about doing the wrong thing with these newly grown-up young men, I might have eliminated his confusion and made him happier by stating, during the winter preceding graduation, that Noah and I would definitely not attend. Noah didn't see things this way. He felt sure that everyone wanted visible proof that he was loved, ". . . and our going to Nick's graduation would show we cared, that we loved him, wouldn't it? Besides, we did love him and wanted to go, didn't we? And those ivied halls . . ."

It would not have been easy, but I could have manufactured some date that we could not avoid, perhaps arranged our holiday abroad so far in advance Noah would have agreed without thinking and then not wished to change it when he realized that it clashed with Nick's graduation. Who knows? But I regret my insensitivity, unconscious though it was. And I learned a lesson—let me say to my own advantage. But I'll go into that in my final chapter, which deals with weddings and other most important matters.

XII

I wish, during those first days that Andrew and I knew each other, perhaps even before his father and I were married, that I had drawn him to me in a giant hug, and told him with no room for doubt that I was not out to take his mother's place. I was Nick and Sam's mother; Cora was *his* mother. That objectively I would treat him the way I treated my sons, ask the same things of him and give to him what I gave them. But I would not ever attempt to displace her; I wanted him to understand, as I did, that he could not love me as he loved her, and should not try. Rather, I hoped that we could be friends.

If I had done this, perhaps the boy's feeling of guilt those times when he did love or like me, and his anguish over divided loyalties, might only have existed, if at all, to a minimal degree and therefore the underlying basis for many of our conflicts would have been removed.

I, in my early thirties at the beginning of my second marriage, did not have the wisdom to do this. Perhaps few of us do. But I urge new stepmothers to think about it and consider proffering to their new stepchildren the actual, articulated expression of a position a child can easily understand: he still has his mother; you are something else, even though you now live with his father—and you do not intend to be the cruel stepmother of the story books.

This piece of wisdom, if such it can be called, only came to me in my late forties, when my stepson and I had worked through many painful years and situations together. Because there had been this guilt, this inability to cope with his suddenly divided world, and because of my limited capacity to help, we still are prey to occasional resentments; hostility can still smolder, or burst actively into flame. But we value each other as people, underneath it all, and always will.

After his graduation from college, Andrew went to Oxford for further work, planning to marry, the next spring, a girl also in academic life. While in England, he wrote me a letter, some of which I quote here:

"I have a very real sense of two things: that the bulk and tangle of our misunderstandings and resentments (for which I am honestly willing to take great blame) are over; and that, of all people in the world, you know me best and see me most clearly for what I am. . . .

"I believe I am marrying a girl who is not terribly unlike you, and qualities I never would have looked for or particularly cherished in another person, I have sought and found in her because of you. Perhaps a fanatical Freudian would make up an elaborate and altogether sordid explanation for this, but I feel that you have, quite simply though with great difficulty, taught me certain values which I would have grown up without. These values are still weak little sprouts in my soil, but they grow. . . .

"I suppose I will wonder for a long time how you managed to care in the midst of all my antagonism and blunt rejection, and all I can really say is that I am grateful for your strength and perseverance and the perverse loyalty of yours which refuses to give up lost causes.

"I hope in the future, that I will repay you in an honest willingness to help in family problems and share in family pleasures. I hope you will lean on me when and if you ever need to and in so doing teach me further the quality of your own fortitude and patience. And I most deeply hope to be a bond and not a bone between you and Dad.

"Please know that the emotion is greater than the words."

I hope Andrew will not object to my exposing his feelings of that time, and will understand, though I have not said so to him, that I think he has been overly generous, and that the blame he refers to must be shared by me.

Because he and Sylvia, his bride-to-be, planned a holiday together abroad before returning to teaching and graduate study in the autumn, the place that seemed most attractive to them for their wedding was London. It so happened that none of their parents (she had four, he three) except Noah and myself, who already had a late May trip to Europe arranged, could make the journey. And so when it came to Andrew's marriage, I was surrogate for three other mothers, Noah for two other fathers. And I have to confess that I thoroughly enjoyed it—it came as an unexpected bonus, since I have no daughters and would not in the natural course of things expect ever to have the joyous task of "putting on" a wedding. I loved the arranging of flowers in the church, our talk with the minister, the consultations with Andrew as to the hotel he should take his bride to, the planning of the small family reception, so beautifully hosted by my English sisters, the buying with Noah of gifts and also the bottle of champagne from Fortnum's which we sent to the hotel. And I began to love the bride, whom I helped dress for the ceremony, properly equipped with "something old, something new, something borrowed, something blue," and who, quite truthfully, was as "pretty as a picture." After Andrew's letter, the entire experience for me could not have been anything but euphoric.

I am not, in this book, going into the relationships of stepmothers and stepsons *after* these particular stepsons marry and have families of their own. But there is one point that I would like to make: there *is* a difference between being a mother-in-law and a stepmother-in-law. Perhaps the stepmother-in-law has less impulse, or likelihood rather, to step on her new daughter-in-law's toes. But once again, she must not usurp the place of the real, natural mother-in-law. It can be a temptation, because the relationship between the two women—stepmother-in-law and stepdaughter-in-law is easier, may well be a more relaxed kind of thing. Before Sylvia and Andrew, in their turn, began having troubles of their own, I felt it necessary (because I wished her to know that I would have preferred it otherwise), to articulate to her that I would like to be much closer to her than I am—for we could be close—but I would not make my stepson feel hurt that it is not his mother who has this ease and intimacy. And so I kept my distance. And she, understanding and agreeing, acted accordingly.

Before he left for overseas, our second boy, Nick, spent several months, off and on, helping Noah and me fix up our new upstate New York farm. It was a rewarding time, in which many differences and prickly problems were smoothed out to the point of disappearance. Nick, grown up, was able to help his stepfather, even teach him certain outdoor skills and help him not to mind when he was unable to do something right the first time, perfectionist that he is (this is hard for my intellectual husband to bear).

We were companions, the three of us, and Noah accepted Nick and valued him as a loved and respected person in his own right, not as a competitive hanger-on to Andrew. Nick, in his turn, pumped Noah for all he was worth, on a veritable encyclopedia of subjects he was interested in and ignorant about, but thought he should know before taking off to other parts of the world. It was a happy time.

Now Nick too plans to marry, a girl he met while on a Fulbright scholarship to New Zealand. And I, finally having learned to be sensitive to his abhorrence of being the focus of interest of two families, wrote him that I didn't think we'd attend his wedding, even if we were able to (which was unlikely). It was one of the most important times in his life, that I wanted him to enjoy and participate in with unalloyed joy—and we would not flaw it in any way. I wrote with no sense of martyrdom or even deprivation, much as I would love to attend and meet Jan (I can hardly wait for this) and her family. But New Zealand *is* a long way off and the fare is astronomically high.

I will now quote part of Nick's letter of response:

"And now about the wedding. I will be very happy if *everyone* (his underlining) can come. I mean it. It would be wonderful if the Joplins and the Links could meet the Henriques and see New Zealand. I know that Jan and her family would be very pleased. And although it is true that in the past I have been sensitive on this matter, in this case I am not uneasy at the prospect, but enthusiastic. This is a far cry from my Harvard graduation, where I *alone* was the object of interest and pride."

But sometimes everyone reverts to childhood patterns, or in my case, patterns that were unhappy-making in the past. And so it is with my stepson and myself. Because Andrew's mother has been so seriously ill, and he therefore is under repeated strains and stresses, supporting in the back of his consciousness a continual worry—the old hostility and sense of guilt and divided loyalty reappear from time to time. I would not expect it to be otherwise, though it makes me unhappy and makes it difficult, perhaps, for Andrew to enjoy our country farm in the companionable, free and easy way the other boys do. Perhaps some of the words of his letter from England and the sentiment behind them must be held in abeyance. It will be like that again. We will work through this period too, and we both know, I believe with all my heart, that neither of us could ever ask for help or reassurance and not receive it. I know that Nick and Sam feel this way about Noah also, and vice versa. I really don't believe Andrew will have to go to jail, like the poor man in Nairobi, for biting off his stepmother's ear!

The step-relationship as a whole tends to get less rocky as one grows older. I would like to say here that the association with our "other parents," the ex-wives and ex-husbands, also improves and is less tense as the children they had in common reach maturity—this, of course only if rags and tatters of old hatred and bitterness have finally been thrown away, like old baggage no longer useful. Obviously, the many problems and issues that they were forced to work out together, hopefully, dealing with money, education, visitation, and so on, as time goes by become fewer and fewer, their relevance to the parents less and less.

The other day I was meeting my father at La Guardia Airport, and Sam, now through college and a "cub reporter," came with me to drive us all home. The plane was delayed, and my youngest son and I went to the fine Restaurant Associates dining room for a drink and a bite.

We talked—among other things of those early days of his childhood in Brooklyn, the train rides to Long Island, his schooldays in New York and at boarding school, and even about my book. It was one of those rare moments when the rapport between two people makes the words they exchange of magic importance. That these words were with my son, now adult, illumined the hour and made it one to be savored, like brandy in a snifter, warmed and treasured, and then held in the heart.

I asked him as I had asked the others, what he remembered, if anything, that was painful, was particularly traumatic. But he could recall nothing of moment, and we agreed that he had experienced the most "normal" childhood of the three.

"Oh, I can remember the Christmases, and

trimming the tree," he said. "And Cindy, and choir practice. And my ninth birthday when I fell over the bannisters from the top floor, and lost my front tooth.

"But troubles? Well, yes, you remember my last year at Gunnery. . . ." And we recalled together a period of contention when Noah and I, as parents, were making demands Sam could not or did not wish to meet, when our relationship suffered. During this time, Sam said, Nick telephoned him from college, and for the first time spelled out for him something that he, Nick, had learned when his parents first separated. He said to his young brother that their parents were like other people, like children even, sometimes right but sometimes wrong as well, with successes and failures and near misses too. They are not gods, and it is not right to so regard them, perhaps it isn't even fair to them, for then too much is expected of them and sooner or later they are not going to be able to deliver.

"This had never occurred to me," Sam said. "I'd always accepted you, and everything you did, before. I found it very useful advice."

We went on to talk more of fathers and mothers, and how a child's role vis-à-vis the important adults in his life changes with his maturity.

"I suddenly realized, just recently," Sam commented, "that it's getting to the time when *I* should be looking after *you*. When I should remember *your* birthday, instead of always the other way around."

I smiled happily at this youngest of my three boys. "I'll look forward to my next," I told him.

Now Sam too comes up to the farm for surcease from his job in the city. He and Noah work together outdoors, chopping, planting a larch forest, planning a pond, with much talk, endless talk, and satisfaction in each other's company. The shared background memories of the same university and the same profession have cemented their affection.

I'm afraid this book must seem very much of a hodgepodge of experiences and advice—sprawling, untidy, unprofessional. It reminds me a little of my sewing box, faithfully though inexpertly used during the years of the boys' growing up. In it were all the necessary items: the pins, snaps, hooks and eyes, darning threads of many colors for socks, superstrong cotton for pea-jacket buttons, scissors and needles, a half-unraveled skein of wool, a thimble, suede elbow patches for my husband and denim ones for the boys' knees, buttons for shirts and shorts, and brass ones for blazers. And above all, mixed in and tangled through the layers of odds and ends were the bundles of name tapes, half unraveled and showing their printed letters: Andrew Joplin in red; Nicholas Links in green; and Samuel Links in blue. Is it not an untidy but cheerful though tangled symbol of our life?

I end with a quote from Willa Cather: "One cannot divine nor forecast the conditions that will make happiness; one only stumbles on them by chance, in a lucky hour, at the world's end somewhere, and holds fast to the days, as to fortune or fame." That is what I am doing, holding fast to these days of happiness. But boys, look out! Just wait until I have grandchildren.